HERE WE GO!

HERE WE GO!

DAWN STALEY'S GAMECOCKS
AND THE ROAD TO THE CHAMPIONSHIP

DAVID CLONINGER | *Photography by Tracy Glantz*

THE
History
PRESS

Published by The History Press
Charleston, SC
www.historypress.net

First published 2017

Manufactured in the United States

ISBN 9781467138604

Library of Congress Control Number: 2017948456

For Marjorie, who inspires me

CONTENTS

1
FINALLY

DALLAS—She sat as she always did.

Dawn Staley watched All-American A'ja Wilson knife through Mississippi State's interior to score with 3:10 to go and didn't scream, clap, celebrate or sigh with relief. She might have known right then that it was going to happen, but there was no way she would ever recognize it. Game wasn't over.

South Carolina's ninth-year coach barely moved—save for pulling her eyeglasses back into place—then returned to the pose she'd adopted while transforming the Gamecocks from a ten-win band of forgotten ladies to the toast of the game. Sitting in her chair, two assistant coaches to her right and one to the left, within three steps of the Wint-O-Green Life Savers she obsessively crunches throughout games that were lined up with military precision on the scorer's table, Staley clutched a rolled-up statistic sheet, with the other hand cupping her fist.

If there were thoughts of how long she'd waited for this, she didn't show it. Perhaps there were memories leading up to the national championship game of the four other times she'd gotten this close—only to go home without. Perhaps she had brooded over all that basketball had given her and how much she had given back as one of the most accomplished and decorated women's players ever yet had never won the national title that was now within her reach.

She was close, damn close, as the best player in the country during her days at Virginia. The Cavaliers reached three straight Final Fours from

1990 to 1992 and advanced to the 1991 championship game but lost to Tennessee in overtime. Staley was named Most Outstanding Player of that tournament, but it was bitter comfort. Best player without a ring isn't anything to boast about.

Her college days ended without—Virginia lost in the NCAA tournament to the team that would eventually win it in every one of Staley's seasons—and she thought her chances of winning a national championship were over. The woman who grew up with a ball in her hand wanted to play forever, but trying to lead other women to a collegiate title had never crossed her mind.

"When I couldn't get it done in college, I thought that was it," Staley said. "I never wanted to be a coach."

But the late Dave O'Brien coaxed her into coaching Temple University in her hometown of Philadelphia, offering the unusual caveat of allowing her to play professional basketball at the same time. That became a run of six NCAA tournaments in eight years but never a trip past the second round.

Another rebuilding job at South Carolina beckoned in 2008, and it took her four years to reach the tournament, seven to reach the Final Four. That again ended in heartbreak, a one-point semifinal loss to Notre Dame sending her home empty-handed. But two years later, here she was watching her Gamecocks play for a national championship against Mississippi State, and that championship was becoming clearer with each dwindling second.

With 2:10 to go, Wilson again found room to score in the paint, and the Gamecocks were up twelve. As the applause mounted and reality set in, Staley rose and walked to the end of her bench, telling her substitutes to be ready. After a timeout, she made the switch, letting her starters be cheerleaders for the final forty-one seconds.

Still no celebrating. Not yet. Still too much to do. Mikiah "Kiki" Herbert Harrigan was about to shoot two free throws, and Staley was coaching her through her form.

Twenty-nine seconds. The Bulldogs were fouled. But unless they had a fifteen-point free throw lined up, the game was over.

Now?

Now.

Staley called her assistant coaches for a group hug on the sideline. Their stoicism broke after the embrace, with Staley smiling as Lisa Boyer adoringly patted her head and rubbed her shoulders. Nikki McCray-Penson wiped away tears.

With ten seconds to go, Staley reverted to Coach Staley, erasing the smile as she approached Mississippi State coach Vic Schaefer at midcourt for a handshake, hug and congratulations. She did the same with each of the despondent Bulldog players.

As she reached the end of the line, Staley heard the USC fight song, saw her players leaping and dogpiling, accepted a brand-new championship ball cap—and finally grabbed the trophy she'd been waiting so long to hold.

So many others who had come before that had pledged to Staley when there was scarce hope that this day could ever come, smiled, laughed, pumped their fists and sobbed. Keish, Newt, Bri, Demetress, Eesh, Charenee, Val, Granny, Ash, Elle, Three-na, Muffin, D, Tiff, Asia and O, all of them were as much a part of it as Lay, B, Ty, Lish, KD and A'ja were now.

The confetti and music and kudos rained, as they have since. The nets came down, one to remain around Staley's neck for most of the next two months, and the championship bauble never strayed far from her hands. Through a seventeen-year professional and Olympic career that solidified her place as a legend and twenty-five years since her collegiate playing career ended without the one prize she wanted so badly, she had it.

Dawn Staley was a national champion.

But one game didn't nearly tell the journey it took to get there.

2

END OF THE BEGINNING

F irst day, last day, it never wavered. Dawn Staley was on the practice court with her team and wanted it to perform an offensive rotation.

To perform it correctly.

"No, you missed the cutter."

"No, you butchered the pass."

"No, no, no!"

More instruction, more command and the constant directive after every break.

"Here we go!"

Eventually, they did it right, and practice resumed. But in mid-October, there were a lot of days left to keep doing it right and a whole lot more to install before they were ready to play a game.

Yet there was something about this squad. Despite losing two-time SEC Player of the Year Tiffany Mitchell, point guard Khadijah Sessions, three-point maestro Tina Roy, three-year starter Asia Dozier and Sarah Imovbioh, who had transferred from Virginia for a final year in Columbia, the Gamecocks looked solid.

Two transfers who sat out the year before, Allisha Gray (North Carolina) and Kaela Davis (Georgia Tech), were eligible. Four freshmen had arrived, plus transfer Alexis Jennings from Kentucky, who could practice but not play in 2016–17.

Gray and Davis's offensive talents could fill a void right away and give South Carolina a devastating four-punch attack in any game by combining with reigning SEC Player of the Year A'ja Wilson and first-team All-SEC selection Alaina Coates. There wasn't a lot of proven depth or experience on the roster—the Gamecocks would suit up eleven maximum for the season, six who had yet to play one minute in a USC jersey—but Staley liked what she saw thus far.

The only question was at point guard, where the Gamecocks had an experienced junior in Bianca Cuevas-Moore as well as a lot of fresh-faced talent. Cuevas-Moore could electrify the Gamecocks with a stunning combination of speed and savvy, but that ability to take over could be as great a curse as it could a blessing—hence the nicknames many on the outside had bestowed upon her Jekyll-and-Hyde game: "Good Bianca" and "Bad Bianca."

"We've got a really good team, but we've got to work through some things," Staley said. "They're a pretty unselfish group right now. We got a little ways to go from a defensive standpoint, but they're eager to learn."

All would be determined in practice before a brutally tough schedule arrived. Staley wasn't going to take it easy on her Gamecocks because they had to grow up sometime, and after the 2015–16 season had resulted in so many wins and such a disappointing finish, a challenging gauntlet of games would hopefully avoid losses when USC really didn't want them.

The Gamecocks, christened the No. 4 team in the country in the preseason, would take on ten other preseason Top 25 teams, beginning on the road against No. 7 Ohio State. Defending national champion Connecticut (3), Louisville (5), Texas (8), UCLA (9), Mississippi State (10), Tennessee (13), Kentucky (19, two games), Florida (20) and Missouri (24) dotted the slate. Auburn (two games), Texas A&M and Duke received votes in the poll as well.

Having proven scorers in Gray and Davis and needing to get points early in the year—USC would play the Buckeyes, Cardinals, Longhorns and Blue Devils within the first seven games, all away from home—had Staley switching it up. A proponent of letting offense flow from defense, a staple that made the Gamecocks one of the country's best at preventing points over the past three years, Staley liked to implement defense first in preseason practice.

This October, she was switching to offense.

"Allisha Gray is probably the one person who's in mid-season form," Staley said. "To have those types of players eligible now, I think it gives us a lot of options. They certainly have done a tremendous job playing with each other."

When Gray and Davis could score inside and out—each filled the bucket from anywhere and became red-hot seemingly at will—and the post tandem of Wilson and Coates had an advantage over anybody they'd play, the Gamecocks had the capability to assert their will early and then let the newbies get their feet wet. USC could simply dominate if it got off to a great start.

Gray had an interesting career. She left North Carolina among a wave of defections—including Diamond DeShields, who visited South Carolina on her way to Tennessee and would face the Gamecocks her remaining two years—and was looking for a new start. She found it with the Gamecocks, an ironic move considering her personal history with them. As freshmen, Gray and DeShields teamed up to knock USC out of the Sweet 16. As a sophomore, Gray sat at a table in Greensboro discussing how USC had just eliminated the Tar Heels in the Sweet 16.

Now, the lights-out scorer and takeover player would be wearing garnet and black for her junior season. She entered a team like she played on at UNC—there were proven scorers, there was experience at point guard. Quiet and understated by nature, Gray might be asked to take over, but if she had to remain the glue of the team in the background, that was fine by her.

Davis was put on the planet to score, which is what she did at Georgia Tech. The daughter of NBA veteran Antonio Davis, Kaela Davis lit up the stat sheets during her two years with the Yellow Jackets, becoming the fastest in school history to break the one-thousand-point plateau. Coming into a team with an established offense—the forwards were relied on for the bulk of the scoring, not the guards—Davis believed she could perhaps handle a reduced role.

"[Being the main scorer] is not even something I want to do, honestly," she said. "Now that I've done it, that is nothing I want to do. When you have 6',4" and 6',5" sitting down there, you're not going to just let them sit down there. When you have that, you want to utilize that. It's making all that work. We have a lot of pieces to work with this year."

The Gamecocks were again picked to win the league at SEC Media Days, with Wilson named preseason player of the year. Coates, who wore two fistfuls of rings to the event, said that it was great to have that recognition but they all had their eyes on another prize: the one trophy at the very end of the season they hadn't yet been able to obtain.

"The anticipation is really high, waiting for the season to get here. I do feel like there's high expectations, I do feel like there's a target on our back," Coates said. "Everybody's gunning to knock us off the SEC championship pedestal we've gotten the last three years and hopefully are going to get the fourth year."

The chemistry was already tight as well, although that hadn't been a problem during Staley's tenure. Winning streaks tend to do that, and no team in program history had been winning like the Gamecocks.

USC set an SEC record in 2015–16 with its forty-fifth conference win over three seasons, also becoming just the second team in history to post a perfect 16-0 SEC season. The Gamecocks, who won all but one game among thirty-two straight regular-season SEC games and two straight SEC tournaments, also tied 2010–11 Tennessee as the only conference teams to go 19-0 (regular-season and tournament champs) in one season.

"This team is way different than the team that we've put on the floor the last few years," Staley told the SEC Network. "Different doesn't always mean bad—it's a different good....When you bring back two of the top forwards in the country, forward-center combination in the country, you can feel really good about what's going to surround them. But there's some question marks coming up with our team, one of them being the point guard position. Another one being, how well will our transfers mesh with the core of our players that are returning?"

Staley had never been shy about taking transfers, but bringing in two who were supposed to heavily contribute right away after being stars at their previous schools was a departure from the norm. Imovbioh had been an elite rebounder at Virginia and was bolstering the Gamecocks' defensive presence in 2015–16, but Gray and Davis were going to most likely start in 2016–17.

The time would come when they would have to score, maybe not as the first two options but as third and fourth. How was that going to work?

"We're at a place where we're sharing the basketball. They're understanding that they have a lot more players around them, and they're doing a great job on both sides of the ball," Staley said. "They're committed to wanting to take this team to winning a national championship. But we also know, it's the innocent time of the year."

Egos would have to be shelved and teamwork built, but that had never been an issue before and wouldn't be this year. Gray and Davis each understood that the Gamecocks had a preferred way to do things and outsiders coming in were welcomed, but they had to earn their stripes.

It was no problem. Gray, as dynamic as a player could be, was a follower much more than a leader. Davis, after two years of experiencing brief postseason runs at Tech and then watching USC lose in the Sweet 16 the year before, was fully invested into helping the team reach its maximum potential.

"I want to be able to compete at a really high level," Davis said. "I want the opportunity to play for a national championship. With that in mind, I think South Carolina was the place to do that."

Brad Muller, the radio voice of the Gamecocks for Staley's entire tenure, saw what he'd seen over the past few years on the first day of practice. There was talent galore.

But talent wasn't everything. USC would need somebody to corral it, coax it into one unit bent on one goal. The Gamecocks had lost a lot of that.

"They didn't have Tiffany Mitchell anymore. That was a big question for me going into the season—who was going to be the leader? Because you can't just tell somebody they're the leader. They have to want it," Muller said.

"I thought it would be A'ja because she had to be. Alaina, the way she played, would have to be one. I wasn't sure because it usually comes from the point guard, but Bianca was really just stepping into the starting role."

Staley had posted the absurd stat of growing her SEC win total in each of her eight years at USC, going from two in 2008–9 to sixteen in 2015–16. Yet as magnificent as the accomplishment was, there was still a hollow feeling from the way last season ended.

It was unfair to label a 33-2 team that was unbeaten against SEC competition as not living up to expectations, but that's what happens when a team wins so often and made it look easy so many times. Staley didn't bring it up as a motivational tactic and the players didn't talk about it on that October day, but the feeling lingered.

What happened in South Dakota? How could the Gamecocks, as superb a team that had ever worn the uniform, lose to Syracuse in the Sweet 16? Why did it all collapse in one forty-minute session—scratch that, a twenty-minute half—when it had been so destined for greatness all year?

"It's obvious we had expectations of going further than the Sweet 16," Staley said a few days after that loss. "But I think that at points throughout our journey, we always have to take a step back—we don't want to, but you have to take a step back to move yourself forward. Looking at how we ended up, we took that step back."

During that 80–72 loss, the Gamecocks were suckered into playing the Orange's way. Syracuse, known for its zone defense, put Mitchell on the bench with two quick fouls and was making it difficult for USC to get the ball to Wilson and Coates. Yet the Gamecocks still led by ten at halftime, due to a sterling three-point shooting exhibition from Roy.

The script was plain as day: USC had taken a punch but would get Mitchell back in the second half and could return to what had made it so superior in SEC play. Get the ball to Wilson and Coates, let Mitchell be Mitchell, get enough from the others and meet Tennessee or Ohio State in the Elite Eight.

Except the players kept shooting three-pointers, only one of which went in. Their rebounding, used to camping under the basket with their twin towers, was seeing those three-point misses become long caroms to the running Orange. Their defense collapsed, and in the fourth quarter, so did their season.

"We took the bait," Staley said. "If you look at our stats, our post players are seventeen of twenty-two from the floor, thirty-one rebounds, thirty-one points. Shooting at that percentage, we should have been trying to get that ball in a lot more than what we did."

Staley had been in this position before, as player and coach, having to gather a shattered team and make it whole again. It was never easy, but it was part of the college game; players come and players go, and sometimes it's not the best team that wins. Sometimes, as Syracuse showed by getting all the way to the national championship game, a team gets hot and plays its best at the end of the season.

As good as the Gamecocks had been since breaking the NCAA tournament glass ceiling in 2011–12, they hadn't gotten the big prize. Staley knew how hard it was but mentioned to her returning players how much they had to work, how much they had to want, in order to get it.

"I told our players, if you're hurting, if you're crying because you're saying good-bye to our seniors, great," Staley said. "But you should hurt and you should cry for not being in this position at this time of the season by the amount of work you need to put in to ensure that this doesn't take place prematurely anymore."

"This program's always done a good job of turning the page," Muller said. "They certainly didn't like it, and they knew they lost to a team they should have beaten, but like everybody does eventually—they were a very talented team that had a bad day."

Everything in the season bleeds into another. The only thing that really matters is getting to the NCAA tournament and finding a way to play in six games, then winning that sixth one. Get that one, and it doesn't matter what a team did before it.

But a team needs to win its rivalry game(s), needs to win the "name" games on its schedule, needs to do well in conference, needs to do well in the conference tournament. That all goes into producing better seeding in the NCAAs and better opportunities, like playing at home for the first two games and perhaps being sent nearby for the next two, so the fans can come along.

The Gamecocks were still devastatingly talented with a one-two punch at guard and heavier one-two volley in the paint. That offensive philosophy—get the ball to the big girl—had been in place since Coates arrived and would remain that way for the next season. Except now, the Gamecocks had two proven scoring guards ready to light it up.

"We got a really good team, but we got to work through some things," Staley said on that first day of practice. "There's a different feel in the gym."

So it was on that long-ago first day, when the only quality the Gamecocks had was hope.

3

SPINNING WHEELS

The situation wasn't good.

Dawn Staley stepped into a program that was coming off three straight WNIT appearances but one whose fewest number of losses over the past five seasons was twelve. After the back-to-back brilliance of 2001–2 and 2002–3, South Carolina had plummeted to earth. The Gamecocks had back-to-back losing seasons where they won a combined three SEC games and then posted two winning seasons and a .500 year before coach Susan Walvius resigned.

The turnover didn't stop there. Leading scorer Jordan Jones transferred to Florida after 2007–8, and while Staley inherited Demetress Adams and Brionna Dickerson, the Gamecocks' No. 2 and 3 scorers, she also lost Nos. 4 and 5 Lakesha Tolliver and Ilona Burgrova.

But Staley added what she could, including a fierce guard from New Jersey named La'Keisha Sutton and enforcer forward Charenee Stephens of Georgia, and went to work.

There wasn't much to expect from that team, and everyone knew it. But Staley was the coach, and while she might have also known that, she would never admit it.

It's why she said the words at that first media day that had everybody wondering, "Huh?"

"Our goal is to get to the NCAA tournament, and the best way to do that is to win your conference. That is what we are shooting for. We want to be the best," Staley said. "We are playing in the underdog role, and we relish playing in that role. Our kids need to have the mindset of winning the Southeastern Conference, and that is what we are going to try to do. Ultimately, our goal is to win a national championship."

Goals are great. Being confident is great. But USC had not exactly blown the doors off the country in the last five years. Walvius guided the Gamecocks to the Elite Eight in 2002 and the NCAA tournament round of thirty-two the next year, success the Gamecocks hadn't seen since their Metro Conference days. But the forty-eight wins over those two years had not been sustained—once that core of Jocelyn Penn, Shaunzinski Gortman and Teresa Jeter left, USC sped faster than Superman back to reality.

The Gamecocks won eighteen games over the next two seasons combined, a measly three in the SEC. Rebuilding might have been expected, and USC did make the postseason in each of the three seasons between 2005 and 2008. Those were WNIT berths, and only one season featured a trip past the second round. After a 16-16 season in 2007–8, Walvius resigned.

"I remember calling a game when I had to be quiet during free throws because they could hear me," said Brad Muller, who took over USC radio during Walvius's last season. "And when I said, 'So-and-so's only a 50 percent free-throw shooter,' that girl turned and looked at me because it was so quiet in the gym she could hear me."

Then–athletics director Eric Hyman, a visionary who saw so much ahead for USC if it would quit feeling sorry for itself and conveniently blame a "chicken curse" for athletic mediocrity, knew who Staley was and had her on his short list, although she was the last of three finalists to interview. Hyman saw Staley play at Virginia and watched her coach at Temple in an NCAA tournament game while he was the athletics director at Texas Christian, but the interview in Columbia didn't go as smoothly as Hyman would have liked.

It took a trip to Philadelphia, where Hyman met Staley on her home turf, the streets and courts where she grew up, for Staley to drop her guard and really get to know the man who wanted her to be his coach.

That was all it took. The mutual interest soon had both parties agreeing to a deal, which at the time paid more per year than baseball coach (and Hyman's successor as athletics director) Ray Tanner was receiving.

The money for a program viewed as a non-contender, sparsely attended even in the good times, was lively message-board talk. "Why spend that kind of cash on a sport that will never turn a profit or generate interest?" the queries moaned.

Hyman, who did things his way and more than any other person transformed USC into a top athletic program across the board, knew he'd found the correct solution. It just might take some time to show it.

(Years later, Hyman asked about Staley and her team first thing during an interview from his athletics director's office at Texas A&M. He never forgot the criticism he heard when he hired her.)

That first season boasted Staley's presence much more than the players on the team. Staley wanted to change that and show she could immediately turn around another program after her first two Temple teams reached the WNIT and the NCAA tournament. That first season, in 2000–2001, was the first winning season the Owls had since 1989–90.

Yet she knew at USC, it would be tough sledding.

"I'm not so much into the win-loss type of results," Staley said. "If we put in the work and compete at the highest level we're capable of, the results will take care of themselves."

The Gamecocks did well in their early season but were blistered at home by No. 3 Stanford and No. 1 Connecticut. Still, they topped NC State by a point on the road and stood 8-5 entering the SEC; perhaps they could make a run at a postseason berth.

"Little games like that, nobody cares or remembers, but that NC State game gave glimpses of greatness that we saw," Sutton said.

USC began 0-4 in the league, but three games were against Top 25 teams, and the other was on the road. They were competitive, losing by four at Auburn, six at Georgia and twelve at Tennessee. A corner was turned with Staley's first SEC win, a 76–67 triumph over Ole Miss.

And then that corner was unturned with a cruel twist.

Adams, the Gamecocks' third-leading scorer and top rebounder, was lost for the season with a knee injury against the Rebels. Three days later, the Gamecocks lost to Vanderbilt, and leading scorer Dickerson went down with a knee injury. She tried to rehab it and get back on the court but was declared out for the year three weeks later.

"They were our two leaders, and just from a basketball perspective, they were our point guard and our main post player," Sutton said. "We were just, 'Now what do we do? How do we continue as if nothing happened, because something obviously did happen?'"

"It forced people like myself to step into new roles."

Sutton, who wound up placing second on the team with eleven points per game, tried her best to rally the troops, but the Gamecocks simply didn't have enough firepower without Dickerson and Adams. USC won only one of its final ten games and finished 10-18.

"You have to play the hand you're dealt," Staley said in a statement, "and we did that. We may have taken a step or two back along the way, but for the most part, for who we had and the lack of experience we had, they played as well as they could play."

"I could sense she was frustrated because she'd been so used to winning. It was different kids. She didn't have the same inner-city tough kids, and then her two best players got hurt in back-to-back weeks," Muller said. "She's a winner, and she wasn't used to losing, especially not how many we lost that first season. I remember her saying something along the lines of 'Basketball gods, what have I done to you?'"

It was a rotten first year, but not many expected different. As much of a program-changer as Staley was, she couldn't get out there on the court and put the ball in the hoop. Players had to do that, and she didn't have many—but she was about to land several.

Staley needed recruits, and she'd already started convincing some of the country's top talent to come be a part of something special in Columbia. Ashley Bruner and Ieasia Walker pledged to give the Gamecocks immediate help, and then Ebony Wilson joined as well. A transfer from Long Island University, Valerie Nainima, would be eligible after sitting out in 2008–9.

On April 15, 2009, it happened.

Kelsey Bone was the No. 2 recruit in the country and could have played anywhere. Most figured she'd stay close to her Texas home.

Instead, she chose USC, giving Staley's project an immediate foundation. If one of the top players in the country would pick the Gamecocks after a 10-18 season, who else would come when they really got going?

"A lot of the load [is] on my shoulders, but I don't feel that," Bone said at her first media day. "It's always kind of been there for me. At the end of the day, it's just basketball. The basketball's just a different level."

Players of her capability didn't come along too often and definitely didn't choose USC. Why did she?

"Going against the grain, I've always kind of been that kid," she said. "We might win a national championship this year, we might not ever win one with me here. But with me coming in and coach Staley and other great players interested in the school, I think the impact has been felt all around the sport."

The 2009–10 season began strong, with Nainima taking the scoring lead and Bone being named SEC Newcomer of the Year. The freshman was second on the team in scoring and tops in rebounding, while Sutton, Stephens and Walker formed a solid nucleus for the future.

USC beat a San Diego State team ranked No. 23 at the time and had close losses to No. 20 Oklahoma and No. 9 North Carolina. The Gamecocks also lost 60–55 to No. 5 Tennessee, the closest margin of defeat that series had seen since 1989.

USC entered February with two straight wins, one at No. 14 Georgia, but dropped back-to-back SEC games by a combined six points. That led to two blowout losses to ranked Kentucky and Georgia before rebounding to beat Vanderbilt in the regular-season finale.

The Gamecocks just missed the postseason, finishing 14-15 after five losses in their final six games, but the coming years were glowing. A one-point SEC tournament loss to Ole Miss on March 4, 2010, stung, but Staley could hardly wait for the next season to start.

"We got to become winners. I don't think our team had that every time we took the floor. At the same time, you know, we did get better," Staley said. "It's hard to see right now sitting here right after a loss in the SEC tournament, but we got better. We're more talented than we were last year. We want to get more talented in the years to come."

Just under a month later, the corner she again thought she'd turned was revealed to be the start of another long sidewalk.

"That's something that Kelsey is probably going to have to talk to you guys about," Staley said. "For us, we just got to keep moving forward. This type of thing happens all the time. It's unfortunate it happened to our program at this time."

Bone wanted to transfer. Staley granted it with no restrictions—Bone wound up at Texas A&M—and while she portrayed it as part of the game that has to be dealt with, there was no mistaking the loss of such a program-changing player.

It removed a twenty-seven-game starter who led all SEC freshmen with fourteen points and 9.2 rebounds per game. It also removed some of the good that had been gained when such a high-ranking recruit had chosen South Carolina, of all places. Perhaps everything wasn't as golden as it seemed.

Or perhaps it was a teenage girl who didn't feel comfortable where she was and wanted to go somewhere where she could be happy.

"We still talk every day," said Sutton, Bone's roommate that season. "Yes, it hurt to lose her but I thought, 'If she doesn't want to be here, why beg her to stay? She's going to be a liability.'…I'm not mad or anything because that girl's like my sister. She felt she needed to leave, and I wished her well. I was focusing on helping my team. I felt like I had to take my teammates' backs."

Bone would be part of a national championship–winning team at A&M, but it was the year she sat out due to transferring. She later declared early for the WNBA and left A&M after her second season.

"You don't want to lose a player like that but at the same time, you want people who want to be here," Staley said. "I think we're in a good place. We've been doing some team-building things, some life skills sessions, that have been going pretty darn good. I like the direction our team is going. We're a much closer basketball team because of this."

What spoke louder was the presence of the remaining Gamecocks who gathered behind their coach during the announcement in a quiet, defiant message. The ones who were still committed to Staley's vision weren't panicking or following Bone's lead.

"We're still here," they said without speaking. "And we're going to be OK."

Would they?

4

SUCCESSFUL FIRST TESTS

Alaina Coates sank two free throws, and South Carolina led by twenty-eight. Against a Louisville team that entered the season ranked fifth in the country, South Carolina was winning in a romp.

In a row of seats stocked with women's basketball writers of the Northeast, one journalist shook his head watching USC effortlessly run, score and defend.

"That's the best team in the country," he said.

To whip Louisville to finish the Basketball Hall of Fame Women's Challenge unbeaten, and to do it on a neutral court in Springfield, Massachusetts, had Dawn Staley feeling very, very good about her team. The Gamecocks began the season with a 92–80 thrashing of Ohio State on the road and then played the first three Challenge games at Colonial Life Arena, overwhelming hapless Hampton, Maine and St. Peter's by an average of nearly forty-nine points. That set up the showdown with the Cardinals, which wound up being not much of one—an eight-point lead at halftime was twenty by the end of the third quarter.

The Gamecocks were simply too much. Louisville counted on its speed to run past defenses and outscore the opponent, wearing down teams with its own All-American, Asia Durr.

They had no solutions on how to handle Coates, A'ja Wilson, Kaela Davis and Allisha Gray.

The twin towers combined for thirty-four points, and freshman forward Mikiah "Kiki" Herbert Harrigan chipped in eleven. Gray had seventeen and Davis thirteen, while USC shot 45 percent from the field. The Gamecocks breezed, 83–59.

Staley loved the offense, but the defense—something that had been a staple of her earlier teams' success—was lacking. "We're getting by with kind of patching it together," she said. "We got to get a little bit more disciplined defensively."

The Cardinals only shot 38.3 percent from the field, but Staley didn't like some of the principles that were taking place on the floor. The Gamecocks always had the shot-blocking tandem of Coates and Wilson, but if her perimeter defenders were being schooled off the dribble and the two bigs were moving around the paint in a man-to-man defense, sometimes they couldn't get back to the rim to block the shot.

Scoring defense was a hallmark of Staley's teams, stretching back to their first NCAA tournament appearance. The 2011–12 team finished fourth in the country in the statistic, a stunning accomplishment after ranking ninetieth the year before.

Since, it had always been good but not as good as that team. The next year was fifth, the next eighth, the next twelfth, the next twenty-fifth. Those were very strong, but thus far in 2016–17, the Gamecocks weren't as tight as they needed to be.

Much of that was the schedule. Against the "test" teams, the Top 25 squads Staley had front-loaded onto the slate, the Gamecocks were allowing healthy shooting percentages. (Ohio State topped the early list at 40 percent.) Against the schedule-fillers like St. Peter's, USC was keeping it under 30 percent.

Tyasha Harris had first taken the assignment of stopping Durr and had done well, denying her the ball and making her work for her touches. Durr only took 10 shots and scored 13 points (she would end the season averaging 19.2 points on 42.4 percent shooting). The Gamecocks switched up their defenses, too, something that would come in handy at the end of the season.

"It's a great start to a tough week for us, and I think our players really enjoy, they focus in a little bit more, when the competition's a little stiffer," Staley said. "We're still in search of who we want to be on both sides of the ball."

They needed to improve on defense, but the way they were scoring was certainly impressive.

The Gamecocks exploded in their opener, taking on Ohio State in a Top-10 matchup in Columbus. Davis poured in thirty-seven points in her first game in over a year, while Gray, the other transfer, added twenty-four.

With such a lethal combination at the guard spots, the Gamecocks barely needed Wilson and Coates, although Coates had her usual double-double with ten points and thirteen rebounds. Wilson, in a rare off night, never got going after early foul trouble. She fouled out with five points and three boards.

"I think tonight with Wilson getting in foul trouble early, that made it kind of difficult to get the ball inside," Davis said. "Tonight was just one of those games where we kind of had to apply ourselves."

She led the charge, slashing through the Buckeyes' zone defense that was designed to take away Coates and Wilson. In a sticky game where fifty-one fouls were called but USC was rewarded more than the home team, had the Gamecocks not missed fifteen free throws, the final score would have been worse.

Davis and Gray scored ten straight points in a stretch after Wilson fouled out, securing the victory. USC was off and running, its two transfer guards giving the Gamecocks a dimension they hadn't had.

"We're not going to be the team we were in the past years where the point guard actually controlled the tempo [and] everything worked through the point guard," Staley said. "We're going to play off what they do best."

The three home drubbings set up the Louisville match, which was again easily handled. Yet Staley kept her foot tapping the brakes—the Gamecocks were about to take two more road trips: Texas and Duke.

The Longhorns were tough but were vanquished in Austin, 76–67. Wilson returned to her All-American self with thirty-one points. Texas crept within four points one minute into the fourth quarter, but Wilson put back a missed Coates bucket with a foul, then propelled the Gamecocks to a seven-point lead.

USC knew what it had the day it signed Wilson, but to see her take over games was still special. The six-foot, five-inch ponytailed whirling dervish seemingly came up with every big play whenever the Gamecocks needed it most, and nobody was going to stop her.

Texas was her first career thirty-point game, but the swatted layup on Longhorn Joyner Holmes with just over three minutes to go was yet another highlight in her budding National Player of the Year campaign. Harris scored four points after that to push the lead into double digits, and the Gamecocks were 6-0.

The Blue Devils, reeling from a rash of offseason attrition, were going to be a challenge but one the Gamecocks could handle. USC had won at Cameron Indoor Stadium two years before in what became a Final Four season, and like then, they planned on turning the arena garnet. Four buses of fans were coming with them.

That 2014–15 crowd saw the first glimpse of what was to come from Wilson and a team that would advance to the Final Four. Trailing one point with less than twenty seconds to play, Staley inserted defensive specialist Olivia Gaines, a junior college find originally from Chester, South Carolina. Gaines ended the game with one minute in the box score, but it was more like seven seconds.

The seven seconds that helped win the game.

Gaines swiped the ball on the sideline from Duke's Rebecca Greenwell and, after thinking of driving for the go-ahead layup, called timeout. USC drew up a play for Tiffany Mitchell, but her spinner into the lane hit side rim and came down.

The rebound came to Wilson, who put it back up with only a couple of ticks to go. The then-freshman got her first taste of being at the bottom of a celebratory dogpile soon after.

This time around, Duke came into the game with one loss (to Vanderbilt) but still looked to be an underdog. Again surrounded by garnet from the visiting fans, the Gamecocks sprinted to an eleven-point lead.

All of the visitors who were cheering so early left disappointed. Duke won 74–63, that swift lead vanishing in a 27–6 Blue Devil run into the second quarter.

"I did something I don't normally do," Staley said. "They got momentum, and we could never get it back." Staley blamed herself for substituting her bench players too early in the game, which triggered Duke's run, and the question from Ohio State and Louisville rose again. USC could score, but how many shootouts could it win? There had to be a stop on defense, and there had to be much more than what the Gamecocks had produced thus far.

Staley acknowledged, "We knew coming into this season that we would take a hit defensively. And sometimes when you're winning, and you're beating top-ranked teams, you can't give that lesson to your players because they just think, 'Hey, we're winning!'"

Duke shot 50 percent from the field—not going to win too many games like that.

"This is a good learning lesson for us," said Wilson, who led USC with eighteen points. "I'm not concerned about this team; I think we have a great team."

The talent was there, but Staley was still discovering who to play where and in what situations. The team's freshmen were coming in just as Gray and Davis had become eligible, and that wasn't easy to handle. They weren't getting as many minutes as perhaps they normally would.

The defense was also being run through far too easily. "We were undisciplined," Staley said, "[an] undisciplined defensive team."

The Gamecocks rebounded to whip Minnesota and Clemson, setting up another Top 10 matchup with UCLA. In Columbia, the Gamecocks struggled to shoot, but the Bruins also couldn't find the nets and USC emerged with a 66–57 win.

The defense was getting better—the Gamecocks wanted to shut down star Jordin Canada and did, Canada scoring fifteen points but shooting a miserable six of twenty from the floor and saddled with fouls. USC also responded to a poor first half with a 15–3 burst in the second half, seizing control of the game. UCLA shot 28.2 percent.

The game was Coates's turn to take control. The senior scored twenty points on ten of fourteen shooting and snared fourteen rebounds, pacing a 24–5 run that salted the game well before the final buzzer. All the Gamecocks worked in tandem, everyone fed off one another and the Bruins were overwhelmed.

That was the plan. As good as the Gamecocks had shown they could be from the guard spots, Coates and Wilson were the crux of the offense. When Coates was unleashed and began to dominate, good luck stopping her.

"She's a beast. She is playing inspired basketball. She is a person that is our aggressor," Staley said. "We look for our players to compete like she competes every minute she's on the floor."

A steamrolling of Savannah State on the road completed the pre-SEC schedule 10-1. The Gamecocks were looking good, taking the lessons from the Duke loss and continuing to apply them. The sixteen-game SEC waited, a crucible USC had navigated to three straight regular-season championships, sixteen straight wins and thirty-one wins in thirty-two tries.

None of that mattered. This was a different team. Living in the past sure didn't help in Durham. "It's a mark of a pretty good team that can play anywhere, any time, and get wins," Staley said. "But not everybody's going to be Top 10. It's those other competitive games, like Duke, that our players don't take as seriously that we have to be concerned about."

The SEC had been the Gamecocks' playground for the past three years, all others allowed inside only with paid admission. A loss at Kentucky in 2015 was the only thorn on a thirty-two-game rose of a run, and USC was bumping Tennessee for historic records set within the league—consecutive wins, consecutive home wins, consecutive championships.

"What we've been able to do in our league the last few seasons makes teams want to beat us and take us down," Staley said. "We got the great players to follow up what we've done in the past, but nothing's going to be given to us."

But like Staley had been preaching since the year began, this was a different team. The non-conference season had shown the Gamecocks, she hoped, that they had to bring it every night. Most nights, their talent would be enough to win.

But they still had to employ that talent and get it to that point. It's not like they were sneaking up on anybody. "It allowed us to focus in on the task at hand, because we had so many competitive games," Staley explained. "It allowed some of the new players to get in the routine of focusing on playing higher competition, and that's what we'll face every night in conference play."

Staley was also considering a change. A point needed to be made.

5

WE ALL WE GOT, WE ALL WE NEED

La'Keisha Sutton wanted out.

"We lost to Ole Miss, and I was just over it," the woman who would become known as Fan Favorite said. "I was trying my hardest, and we kept losing. I hate losing. The mentality of our team was, 'Good try.' Where I come from, it's not like that. We play to win."

Raised in hardscrabble Trenton, New Jersey, Sutton was a late addition to Dawn Staley's first recruiting class. The similarities were obvious and fitting: both came from rough neighborhoods where they spent every second they could on the nearest basketball court, both were guards who burned to win and both found their way to South Carolina.

Staley knew she'd signed up for a rebuilding project that might take years. Sutton had no idea who this lady was, what her program was about or where the University of South Carolina was.

"To this day, Dawn Staley still owes me an official visit to campus. I tell her that every time I come back. 'You just called my stepdad, and I ended up here a day later!'" Sutton reminisced. "Everybody else got the princess treatment. I just showed up right after my prom. I got there and got a call, 'Hey, meet us on the track at six tomorrow morning,' and I was just like, 'Yo, I just finished high school yesterday!'"

Sutton wasn't exaggerating. She wanted to stay in New Jersey and play at Princeton. She didn't know who this Staley woman was, telling her how great she could be. She didn't know how amazing Staley had been on the court; she just had her stepdad's gushing words to her after he got that call.

Grueling strength work and conditioning. Practices where Sutton, being as savvy a point guard as her teacher, picked up what Staley was stressing right away while the rest of the team had to hear it four or five times before it clicked. Yet when they screwed up, it was Sutton's fault. Learning about a different culture and atmosphere while she was in it, instead of being able to ease into it, was awful.

It was a team made up of Susan Walvius's leftovers and whoever Staley could find in the short recruiting period she had when she was hired. Five newcomers joined, only two of whom would last (Sutton and Charenee Stephens).

Call it kismet or history being made or probably mostly what it was—a hardened New Jersey native refusing to back down—but Sutton battled through it.

"My first impression was, 'What am I doing here?' Second was, the off-the-court stuff, the conditioning, it was too hard. I was really struggling," she said. "Practices, the only person that understood as quickly as she wanted us to was me. I was just trying to figure out how to get by each day."

Sutton was developing as a strong player, and Staley saw her as a terrific supporting cast for her two stars. She'd be the player she could build around in the future.

That got fast-tracked and then some.

"We didn't have to start over, but we did have to rely more on outside shooting," Staley said. "We didn't have a steady low-post threat. Demetress [Adams] attracted a lot of attention even if she wasn't scoring. Losing her took a big piece of people concentrating on her and giving us uncontested outside looks. Now those shots were contested, and we didn't have Brionna [Dickerson] to shoot them. We asked C.J. [Pace] to do a lot more scoring, and we put a ton of responsibility on La'Keisha."

When Dickerson and Adams were lost for the season, Sutton was turned to as the captain of a desperate and flagging team. She tried, goodness, how she tried, becoming the SEC's highest-scoring freshman in conference games and never shirking her duties at the point, dishing fifty-one assists for the year. Fans wrote to her praising her determination to make the Gamecocks something they, frankly, weren't.

Sutton was a unanimous SEC all-freshmen team selection, and Staley called her the lone bright spot of the season. That wasn't enough.

"I wanted to go back to New Jersey," Sutton said. "I had my room packed up and everything."

She did like Staley, and she did think the Gamecocks would win—eventually. But losing wears anyone down, especially a freshman seven hundred miles from home.

"My mom told me, 'You're not leaving Dawn Staley,'" Sutton said. "My mom knew I was serious. She was like, 'Keisha, that's normal.' I'd never been to a college before, let alone college athletics. Everybody else was three hours from home, and I was fourteen hours from home. I'm seventeen and doing Olympic drills and WNBA drills and not even knowing how to do them. I was the leader because I scored the most, but I was looking for somebody to lead me."

Staley got word of her star's desperation and held an emergency sit-down with her. She knew help was on the way but had to convince Sutton of that.

The trust won. Sutton hadn't listened to others telling her that homesickness was normal, that she'd eventually make friends, that the drills Staley learned in the WNBA and Olympics would become easier.

She listened now.

"It was more of a, 'Listen, just trust me, I'm going to get better people, people that play like you, fast-paced and creative,'" Sutton said. "She just kept telling me, 'Trust me and trust the process.' And she was right."

The rising sophomore looked at the coach, who earnestly looked at her, and thought of what she'd begun saying to her team before every game, despite the eye-rolls.

"I'd always say that before we came out of the tunnel, in our huddle," Sutton said. "'We all we got, we all we need!' Back then I got a lot of, 'That's corny, that's boring,' but I really felt that way. We didn't have All-Americans; we didn't have Top-10 players. It was just us."

It was Keish who rallied the team together during that rotten first season, Keish who shrugged over Kelsey Bone's transfer after a 14-15 record the next year, figuring the Gamecocks had Stephens to replace her. Sutton knew USC had pieces in Ieasia Walker and Valerie Nainima and that next year wouldn't be as destitute as people thought, even when Nainima blew out a knee over the summer. (She returned that season but wasn't the scorer she had been.)

"We all we got, we all we need!" became a rallying cry for Sutton and the team, something Sutton would write on her sneakers and shout three times before taking the court, her followers loyally chanting it back to her. The Gamecocks may not look that intimidating, Sutton thought, but just wait until the ball's tipped.

"Nobody thought we would win but us," Sutton said. "You know how you look at the other team and say, 'Damn, she's tall. Damn, she's good!' Well, I thought, 'Damn, they got to guard me.'"

They won eighteen games that year—a Herculean accomplishment considering what had gone on during the offseason—and were sniffing an NCAA tournament berth until back-to-back overtime losses to close the regular season crumpled their record. Still, USC made the WNIT and won a game before bowing out, and the future looked golden.

There was a brief hiccup after that season, when Debbie Ryan stepped down after coaching Virginia for thirty-four years. Staley was thought a natural candidate for the job.

The season ended, and Staley responded, "That's the plan," when asked if she'd be at USC next year. The mission had not gone as smoothly or advanced as quickly as she would have liked, and Virginia was home. Why not go?

Why? Because it didn't feel right.

"I figure it was a natural thing for everyone to think the call would be made and that I would be a successor," Staley said. "Looking at it, I see Virginia as probably the only other place I could be passionate about, just because of my association there. I did tell them if I got the call, I had to talk with Virginia. It wasn't a set-in-stone thing, that I was automatically going to be leaving. I think it was my duty to answer the call."

But there was so much at USC that was about to pay off. The next season stood to be a fine one, and the recruiting cycle that was about to start featured numerous Top 100 prospects all within a two-hour drive. Home was home, but Columbia had become home, too.

Was it worth it to give that up and start over again?

"I wasn't worried," Sutton said. "She had said this is where she wanted to be."

Nothing materialized between Staley and Virginia. Then Staley offered a comment that kept repeating itself with each passing year. "It's a gold mine [here]," she said. "I think the foundation's laid; now it's time for us to build a house. A big house."

That declaration elevated the Gamecocks from a spec house to a mansion. Recruits were starting to notice what USC was doing and giving Staley much more than a polite thank-you when she came around with a scholarship offer. They had reached the postseason, and while it wasn't the one they wanted, they could see the next step right in front of them. Sutton would return and lead a tremendous group of veterans who had been through the hard times and knew what it took to win. This next team had the capability to jump-start the project Staley thought would be in motion as quickly as it was at Temple.

Although another slight change was in store. Staley never hesitated to tinker and re-invent and construct an offense or defense to suit her team. There was a delicate balance between what she wanted the players to do and what they could do, but she often walked it.

There was one other adjustment to make.

Practices during those first few years were excruciating, with Staley suffering from Michael Jordan Syndrome. The best each ever was as a player, Staley and MJ couldn't understand why the players they were now in charge of couldn't do it like they could.

Sutton took all the criticism and fired it right back. It was not without repercussions—she probably still holds the unofficial record for number of times getting booted out of practice—but with a lot of production included. There was too much in common to be truly frustrated.

"I could look at her dead in the eye and not wince," Sutton said. "Coach was like, 'I'm gonna send you back to Trenton,' I was like, 'I'm waiting for my plane ticket.' She'd just say, 'You remind me of myself, so much.'"

Sutton talked to Staley and told her that the team might respond better if there was less screaming and more coaching. The Gamecocks weren't like Staley's teams at Temple.

"'Coach, I can take it, but everybody else can't take it,'" Sutton recalled. "'You got to figure out a way to let us mess up and not be perfect.' She started laughing more in practice, trying half-court shots at the end. She gave us a chance to mess up and hold each other accountable."

"We were on a double road trip, staying on the road after playing miserably in the first game. Practice the next day wasn't going well, and I remember coach being very loud in practice and the team just didn't respond, they were all looking at the floor. And I think she knew then that it wasn't working. It wasn't coming across to them," announcer Brad Muller said. "She kind of calmed down and said, 'OK.' Instead of yelling, she explained what she wanted. It was a learning moment for her that not every kid is going to be what she had at Temple.

"La'Keisha was tough and wasn't afraid of anything on the court and wasn't afraid to have an attitude. Not a disrespectful attitude, but the kind of attitude of, 'I can take whatever you dish out.' Dawn learned not everybody has that, and she had to adjust her style. From that moment, we took off."

Team-building became a staple of offseason workouts and created a bond between everyone. Coaches were as much a part of the hugging, crying and giggling as the players.

"From there we said, 'Let's make this thing happen,'" Sutton remembered. They only needed one more piece.

6

SWITCH

ianca Cuevas-Moore hadn't been bad, necessarily. She'd been quite good, actually, over South Carolina's first eleven games.

The cat-quick junior was as renowned for her speed as much as her ability to rally the Gamecocks when they really needed it. Coming into the 2016–17 season, after two years of understudying Khadijah Sessions, Cuevas-Moore was ready to step into one of the most difficult and most thankless positions on campus—strike that, in the country.

It's not that Dawn Staley doesn't love her point guards. Quite the contrary. She knows the skill, leadership and moxie, that "want-to" attitude that all great point guards have. She knows it because that was her as she became the best to ever play it.

There will never be another one like her, and Staley knows that, but it's tough for her to sometimes understand that when relating to her point guards. On a campus that had ten seasons of Heisman Trophy–winning quarterback Steve Spurrier questioning why QBs under his care couldn't perform like he could, it was exactly the same on the basketball court.

I could do it this way, why can't you?

The answer—"I'm *not* you"—was often thought and never said. Staley had to come to that realization and answer it for her point guards. So she began letting them do what they did best, tailoring the offense around what they could do and how they could distribute, and a fantastically successful era began.

Cuevas-Moore, a McDonald's All-American from the Bronx, was the heir to Sessions, a three-year starter from Myrtle Beach who shelved a dynamic scoring career in high school to be a steady floor general for Staley. As a freshman, Cuevas-Moore had shown flashes of what she had done in high school and what she could do in college, and it was always a blazing comet. Nobody, not one player in the country, could keep up with her on the fast break.

The problem was that spark of light was so often a road flare, a bottle rocket that was loud and impressive but only for a brief moment. Cuevas-Moore's brilliance at times was equaled—not surpassed, but equaled—by head-shaking frustration at others.

That speed could so easily be turned into a soaring layup—or a rejected shot to start an opponent's fast break. Cuevas-Moore could put on that fancy two-step dribble up top to start an easy possession or watch it get tipped, plucked and stolen away for two points on the other end.

Those were the times when one mistake often became two, and Staley had to readjust on the fly, her plan to give her starter a few minutes breathing room no longer functional. That was when everyone was thinking, "If she doesn't figure out how to do this soon, the Gamecocks are going to be in trouble."

But those other times. Man, those other times.

USC doesn't make it to the 2015 Final Four without Cuevas-Moore's heroics against Florida State, and if she doesn't steady a floundering ship against Notre Dame in the national semifinal, it's a blowout loss. Remember?

The Seminoles were crushing USC in Greensboro, North Carolina, the Gamecocks unable to stop the drives to the basket or get a handle on the outside shooters, forgetting the kick-out pass when they did manage to shore up the paint. Staley rolled the dice and sat the veteran Sessions, hoping like hell the Cuevas-Moore she had recruited—not that other version—would show up.

If anyone ever looked like she was just waiting to call a timeout, it was Staley right then. Folks swear she had "Tiiiimmmmeeee…" hovering on her lips as Cuevas-Moore got the ball right on the sideline, FSU's Leticia Romero right there with her and the Gamecocks on the bench, half a foot from their teammate with the ball, imploring her to do something.

Cuevas-Moore, salivating over the one-on-one matchup, raced step-for-step with Romero down the floor, dribbling all the way. She sliced through the Seminoles' interior like a witch on her broom, finger-rolling the ball through the basket.

Next possession, she did the same, twisting that windup car body through the trees of FSU's defense, throwing the ball high off the window and through.

The freshman scored nine points in the first half and nearly wiped out a nine-point deficit by herself. She only played two minutes the rest of the game, but her first-half burst was enough.

"I kind of did want to turn the game around," Cuevas-Moore said. "I know what I'm capable of doing, so yeah, that's what I came out and did."

Staley never had to use that timeout. "Bianca is a competitor," Staley said. "Whether she's flying around the court, whether she's having great games or not-so-great games, she's a competitor. But still, even if she doesn't play a minute, if she plays twelve minutes, you know she's always going to be a threat on the floor."

Against Notre Dame in the Final Four, the Gamecocks were about to be blown off the court. Trailing 17–5, Staley again inserted Cuevas-Moore and watched the freshman lead the Gamecocks back into the game, stabilizing the offense although she didn't score much.

The nicknames "Good Bianca" or "Bad Bianca" were used often, and often used several times per game. That was the eyebrow being raised before the 2016–17 season ever began.

Had she learned enough in two years so she could be the point guard the Gamecocks needed?

Through eleven games, the answer was yes. Cuevas-Moore was averaging 6.7 points in 19.1 minutes and had twenty-six assists to fifteen turnovers. She'd only missed one start—freshman Tyasha Harris started against Minnesota, after the loss to Duke—but Cuevas-Moore had been right back in there against Clemson, UCLA and Savannah State.

She looked good. Cuevas-Moore was leading the team with twenty-two steals and had calmed down her "Bad Bianca" moments. Yet as the Gamecocks prepared for conference play, Staley saw something that could perhaps work a little bit better.

USC's defense wasn't as tight as she would like. Cuevas-Moore was an excellent defender, and if she could bring that off the bench when the starters weren't doing well, a message could be relayed for the starters to pick it up.

Plus, Cuevas-Moore was a fine distributor but a really fine scorer. With A'ja Wilson, Alaina Coates, Allisha Gray and Kaela Davis around her, the Gamecocks weren't going to have shots for everybody.

Maybe this could work. While every league game is hard, the Gamecocks had a six-game SEC journey before their first "big" game of the season (Mississippi State, January 23). They already had eleven games against great competition behind them and knew what could work—so why not try something else that could work?

USC took the court for its SEC opener against Alabama. Starters were announced at Colonial Life Arena, and Harris was at point guard.

"Right now, I think we're going to try something a little bit different, try to get some bang off the bench with Bianca," Staley said. "Give her an opportunity to not have so much pressure on her. Ty's more of a pass-first point guard—I think it just fits our style in the beginning of the game."

"I think at first it was kind of a shock, she was used to starting and being in that role. Once Khadijah left, she felt that was her role," said program great Tiffany Mitchell, who counseled Cuevas-Moore during the season from overseas. "But at the same time, she sacrificed for the better of the team to come off the bench. I think it definitely helped her. She embraced her role as well, and that's what you need to do to win championships."

Staley made it clear that the move was not a demotion. Cuevas-Moore was a starter in every sense except for her name not being read with the rest of the starting five. And she also ended the 93–45 demolition of the Crimson Tide (where Harris had seven points and six assists, Cuevas-Moore nine and one) with a warning.

"But if Ty doesn't get the job done, we got to keep moving on," she perilously said.

Harris, from Noblesville, Indiana, naturally grew up with basketball in her veins and had been a finalist for Miss Basketball as a senior. She led Heritage Christian School to three straight state championships, became the Eagles' career leader in scoring and steals and won a gold medal with the under-sixteen Team USA squad in the summer of 2016.

The No. 27 recruit in the country and the No. 8 point guard, all Harris was being asked to do was lead a Top 10 team picked to go to the Final Four to a fourth-straight SEC championship under a coach famously demanding of her point guards. No pressure.

"They told me, 'You know what you're doing. You know all the information, so just take turns and say what needs to be done,'" she said later in the season. "They have confidence in me, so I just have to go do it."

Over the next eight games, she went and did it. Harris started seven of the first eight games of the SEC schedule, all USC wins, and averaged 3.25 assists per game with 15 total turnovers. She could score—putting eleven on the board against Georgia—and she grew every game in her role as the conductor of the Gamecocks' offensive orchestra.

Cuevas-Moore began to flourish as a scorer, pumping in twenty-five points in a three-point win over Georgia, including ten straight at one point, and seventeen more against LSU (where she also briefly re-took the starting role). Staley sometimes had both on the floor together, shocking opponents with their speed and fluidity as they relentlessly attacked the rim and turned nearly every mistake into another Gamecock opportunity.

Fourth-ranked Mississippi State arrived, undefeated and one spot above the Gamecocks in the national polls. The Bulldogs lost the SEC tournament championship to USC the year before and had their greatest season—to that point—end with a sixty-point blowout to Connecticut in the Sweet 16. Yet it was a team brimming with talent. Coach Vic Schaefer had come from Texas A&M, where he was known as "Minister of Defense" for his ball-hawking teaching style, and won the services of Mississippi native Victoria Vivians as his first prep All-American.

Vivians was surrounded by experienced, superlative talent but was facing the Gamecocks at Colonial Life Arena. USC didn't need Chelcie Ross playing Dan Devine in *Rudy* to know the stakes. ("Remember…no one, and I mean no one, comes into our house and pushes us around.")

The teams went back and forth before the Bulldogs took a 35–28 lead at halftime, the Gamecocks shooting a whopping 55 percent but turning the ball over eleven times. That gifted MSU twelve points.

But a 10–2 run out of the locker room fueled by Gray gave the Gamecocks the lead, and they kept finding the buckets to sustain it, answering every Bulldog basket with one of their own. Gray hit a jumper with the ensuing free throw for a 49–48 lead going into the fourth, and when Harris hit two free throws for a 60–57 lead, USC could see the victory.

It didn't last, Breanna Richardson scoring after a Davis foul. Nursing a 60–59 lead, Harris was dribbling time, looking for a bucket to extend the lead with less than a minute to go.

She nearly threw away the game and quite possibly her starting position.

Harris thought she saw an opening and passed the ball, only to see Vivians easily pluck it and take off. Harris chased as Gray ran in stride with Vivians, arms up as she vainly tried to get a hand in Vivians's face.

Gray didn't touch the ball, didn't touch the player. Yet somehow Vivians missed the bunny layup, and Wilson was there to gobble the rebound. Gray missed a transition three-pointer, but Coates laid in the putback for a three-point lead.

Following an MSU timeout, Davis unthinkingly fouled Vivians on a three-point attempt. Vivians swished the first two but missed the third; coach's daughter Blair Schaefer found the offensive rebound and hoisted a three-pointer. That didn't go, Richardson rebounded to give MSU another shot and the Bulldogs again called timeout.

The third time wasn't the charm. Vivians missed another shot, and Wilson rebounded, Morgan William hurriedly fouling her. No way Wilson was going to miss in the clutch—her two free throws cinched a 64–61 win.

"It was just a great feeling, honestly," she said. "This was a very emotional game for us."

USC exhaled. The team had turned the ball over fourteen times and won. It had been out-rebounded on its home court and won. It had gotten the benefit of the whistle—MSU made a scant three of nine free throws, while the Gamecocks converted twenty-one of twenty-eight—and won. It had gotten lucky three times in the final few seconds when MSU had three chances to win—and won.

"I hope that this puts us on edge, because this isn't the end," Staley said, thanking the Lord for making it a home game. "Everybody's still going to give us their best effort. They did get some good looks, but any other place, we lose this basketball game."

The Gamecocks were headed once more toward an 8-0 SEC mark at the halfway point of league competition, with more and more weapons being identified. They were again nearing the top of the mountain.

A rocky peak loomed.

7

MONEY TEAM

I t's different in women's basketball. In men's basketball and the vicious world of men's basketball recruiting, the Top 100 prospects ranked by any of a dozen scouting services are fought over like a T-bone thrown to a pack of wild dogs.

In women's basketball, there are recruiting battles, but a Top 100 prospect—say, one checking in at No. 75—may not be as hotly pursued as No. 75 on the men's side. They'll receive interest, surely, but after the top forty or fifty players commit, recruiting is usually won by which school is closest to the prospect's home or which school is offering, period.

Aleighsa Welch, tabbed "Muffin" by her mother at birth as a shortened version of "my little chocolate chip muffin," was a very strong prospect. Rated the No. 88 recruit in the country, the six-foot forward led Goose Creek High School to its first state championship (beating Spring Valley High and future Gamecock Asia Dozier in the title game) as a junior and another state championship appearance as a senior (where Dozier avenged the loss from the year before). Named South Carolina's "Miss Basketball," Welch was considering offers from Clemson, Georgetown and Virginia Tech until Dawn Staley called.

"It was the day after we won state," Welch said. "She called and said, 'We want to offer you a scholarship.' I was like, 'Who? Me? What?' The serious interest started after that."

Ratings and rankings weren't thought of, although it's never a bad thing to attach "Top 100" to a prospect's name. Welch also appealed to Staley for her relentless energy on the court.

She never saw a rebound she couldn't grab or a defense she couldn't crack. Score, assist, handle the ball, block shots—Welch was the perfect piece to get Staley's project off the ground.

Then there was the other factor. Welch was homegrown, a Palmetto State product. Incredibly, Staley had coached three seasons at South Carolina without recruiting one scholarship player from the state. She inherited South Carolinians Brionna Dickerson (Columbia) and Demetress Adams (Bishopville) on her first team and walk-on Imani Sellers (Holly Hill) joined the team for the 2010–11 season. Welch was the first native daughter Staley landed.

Welch was named the top player in the state and broke the streak of in-state players heading out of state for college. With a bevy of local talent following her, it was an opportune time for Staley to get a "Yes."

"She's an outstanding recruit, and she'll always hold a special place for us because she's our first homegrown recruit," Staley said at the time. "Aleighsa is the kind of player that can make an immediate impact."

Welch heard all of it and wasn't fazed. Staley had said the same to her during her recruitment. If there was pressure to perform, she certainly didn't feel it.

"She sold it to me," Welch said. "That honestly was the selling point: 'Be my first in-state recruit. Be the first to bring it in from in-state. It just takes one. It just takes one to keep in-state talent. Everybody else will follow.' I enjoy being different. I wanted to be that one. I thought, 'We can start showing it's cool and it's OK to stay home and play at South Carolina.'"

Welch joined a freshman class that included Tina Roy (quickly nicknamed "Three-na" for the way she could strafe the basketball from the perimeter) and Elem Ibiam, a six-foot, three-inch center from Georgia. They joined an array of talent that, led by seniors, had bonded over the past three years to become a formidable group.

Nobody was expecting much, which made it loose-knit—at least, as loose-knit as a team could be with a hall-of-famer coaching it.

"We came in with no expectations," Welch said. "My first year, we just wanted to out-work everybody. We prided ourselves on that. And me as a freshman, I just played. I wasn't the smartest kid, but I played hard."

It didn't take long for the returnees to see what they had in their new power forward. Sutton, used to running the offense through the guards, realized the Gamecocks would be much more difficult to defend now that they had a solvent post game.

"What I loved about Muffin was her athleticism," Sutton said. "Her leadership, she was vocal. She was quiet because she looked at me as a leader, but she was vocal. I'm mad because I wish I could have played with her for four years."

"As a former rugby player, I appreciate the way Aleighsa Welch played, every minute. She wasn't intimidated by anyone," announcer Brad Muller said. "Talk about people who have a basketball IQ—she just got it. She was very athletic … not the most athletic person we've ever had, but boy, she just used everything she had on every play."

The Gamecocks got to work after a bit of preseason foreshadowing. Staley ordered the Floyd Mayweather–Victor Ortiz fight on pay-per-view and invited the team to come watch it with her. Sutton, who was already responsible for the Gamecocks' rallying cry ("We all we got, we all we need!"), borrowed a nickname from Mayweather, who claimed another welterweight belt that night.

"Floyd went by 'Money,'" she said. "That was his thing, that to get money was to be valuable and be profitable. So we were the Money Team."

The season started with a win at Illinois (and against future South Carolina assistant coach Jolette Law, in her last season as head coach of the Fighting Illini). Wins over Alabama A&M and Clemson followed before a five-point loss to No. 11 Penn State. USC responded with three more wins (College of Charleston, Presbyterian and Xavier).

The Xavier win was big at first glance. The Gamecocks went on the road and knocked off a team that had gone 29-3 the previous season, including a nineteen-point win over USC in Columbia. But the Musketeers lost coach Kevin McGuff to Washington during the offseason and were embarking on a miserable 8-20 season; the Gamecocks' signature victory became less impressive by the day.

USC fell by two points at NC State before beating Furman and SC State. USC was 8-2 but knew it was going to need some help on its non-conference résumé, and there was scarce opportunity to do that with just three games remaining. Savannah State probably wouldn't help, and even a game at Drexel wouldn't be much better.

But there was that other one. Eighteenth-ranked North Carolina waited in Myrtle Beach, part of a holiday basketball classic the city put on every year.

"I think that was a little bit of a turning point for us," Sutton recalled. "At the time, we were beating the teams we were supposed to beat, but we really didn't have that big win. We needed something to really show ourselves off."

They found it.

The Gamecocks trampled the Tar Heels 79–48 in front of a large garnet-and-black crowd that followed the team from Columbia, their third-largest win over a Top 25 team in program history. USC put on such an offensive clinic that its halftime total (fifty points) would have won the game.

USC shot 47.1 percent and had the Tar Heels down early with an 11–0 barrage. While UNC, the country's highest-scoring offense coming into the game, eventually fought back, that initial burst was too much to overcome.

The Gamecocks shot and hit and shot and hit until their white uniforms glowed red-hot. Sutton scored twenty-one points while Markeisha Grant had twenty, and they managed to out-rebound the superior-height Heels by seventeen. This was the kind of win Staley was looking for and the kind of flow and confidence she needed her team to exhibit. No more could the Gamecocks be taken lightly.

"When you have it going, you just have to let your kids play," she said then. "We just let them play."

And yet what spoke the loudest was how USC approached it afterward. It was a big win, one of the biggest the program had had in decades. Yet the seniors knew there was a long way to go.

"Biggest?" Stephens replied. "It feels good to finally get this win and show them that we came to play. But this isn't the season right here today."

The Gamecocks received votes in the next Top 25 poll but weren't quite in the rankings. They'd get there after five more wins, a position they'd hold for the great majority of the next five seasons.

One of the few times they'd slip out was immediately after they'd gotten there. The five-game winning streak, featuring a 3-0 start in the SEC, quickly became a three-game losing streak. USC wasn't losing by much, but still losing, and another line had to be drawn.

"The easiest thing to do is feel sorry for ourselves and think we can't pull ourselves out of this," Staley said. "Mental, physical [fatigue], the fact that we're losing…it doesn't help our morale. But at the same time, this team is resilient."

USC broke the losing streak with an overtime win at Vanderbilt and returned home for two straight wins over the SEC Mississippi schools, then headed back on the SEC road. Like the North Carolina game, this offered the chance for a signature win. Unlike that one, which was played on a neutral court in-state, there was virtually no chance to win.

The Gamecocks hadn't beaten Tennessee since 1980, which was the only time they'd beaten the Vols. They played sparingly through the 1980s, as USC was an independent and then joined the Metro Conference, but since joining the SEC, the Gamecocks had to play the Lady Vols at least once a year.

Tennessee had won forty straight games over USC—most convincingly so. When Tennessee took control of this game for a 57–50 lead with less than five minutes to play, hey, it's Tennessee, right? Just try to win the next game.

The Money Team never thought that way.

Ieasia Walker laid in a ball from the back side to snap a Lady Vol run, and Grant, playing the finest game of her career, stroked a three-pointer to cut the lead to two points. Tennessee stretched the advantage to five points with 3:37 to go, but USC found forward Ashley Bruner for two points and then Welch in transition for two more.

Thompson-Boling Arena wasn't nervous; the orange-clad heroines had been in plenty tougher situations than this and had won. Staley, with Tennessee's 1991 national championship banner mocking her as it fluttered above, didn't say anything to her team except what it would do on the next possession. Offense, defense. No need to bring up past history.

The Gamecocks took it upon themselves to make it and break it.

Welch soared for a rebound off a missed Tennessee shot and got the ball to Walker, who dribbled down court, stopped and drained a jumper to push USC ahead, 61–60. Walker got to the free-throw line a second later and hit, giving USC a two-point lead with sixty seconds to go.

Tennessee wanted the death strike and went for a three-pointer. It rimmed out, and USC tussled for the rebound. Whistle blew, arrow to the Gamecocks, forty-six seconds left.

Grant had an open look from three but missed, yet Sutton, Trenton toughness trumping Tennessee's talent, grabbed the carom. She was fouled and sent to the line for a one-and-one.

How many times had she waited for this? To be here, her team counting on her, to get that big win? How much had she yearned for it over the past three years when there simply was no hope or opportunity for the Gamecocks to come this far?

All of it flashed through her head as she prepared to shoot the biggest free throws of her life. The Lady Vols gave her extra time to think, calling two timeouts to ice the shooter.

Sutton didn't freeze. Given the ball and a chance to end it, the Gamecocks' captain did what she was counted on to do.

Swish. Three-point lead.

Swish.

Game over.

USC celebrated on the court and throughout the ride home, knowing it had taken another step. For the first time, Staley's Gamecocks could be talked about as an up-and-coming team, an NCAA tournament probable. Wearing a shirt the next day that said, "I Believe," Sutton was asked if she felt the Gamecocks could beat anyone.

"I think I always felt like that," she replied.

The regular season ended with ten SEC wins, tying the most the program ever had, and while the Lady Vols got revenge in the SEC tournament, eliminating the Gamecocks in the semifinals, USC was ready for the next step.

With twenty-three wins, USC was easily an NCAA tournament team. The Gamecocks knew it and invited their fans to a watch party at Colonial Life Arena, a practice that would become standard over the next five years. The NCAA Selection Show began, the first bracket was announced and there it was.

The Money Team cashed in.

The Gamecocks leaped on one another as applause enveloped them, their first NCAA bid since 2003 sending them to West Lafayette, Indiana, to play Eastern Michigan. Grant, Sutton, Ebony Wilson, Courtney Newton and Stephens embraced it the most, knowing their final years of eligibility would be spent driving a stake in the ground, separating USC's struggling past from a future that was fiercely glowing.

"For me as a coach, I envision our program being a part of NCAA tournaments," Staley said then. "Didn't think it would take four years, but it was well worth the wait."

"The ten years doing radio here and thirteen years at Georgia College, that first NCAA tournament team is one of my favorites of all time because they had such great chemistry," Muller said. "They were talented, because you don't win twenty-five games by accident. Everybody was happy with their role. Everybody played much bigger than they were. They knew what they wanted to do and went out and did it. They got where they were on hard work and chemistry."

Eastern Michigan was a warm-up, an 80–48 demolition that advanced the Gamecocks to the Round of 32 to play Purdue, the host. A physical game awaited, but USC didn't have much trouble with the Boilermakers, sending the Gamecocks to the Sweet 16 for just the third time in program history.

They were dispatched to Fresno, California, to take on Stanford and their twin towers, Nnemkadi and Chiney Ogwumike. Refusing to let it end, USC gave the Cardinal everything it had, but it became a simple matter of height—the Ogwumike sisters, especially Nnemkadi, were bigger than USC's forwards. Get them the ball.

Stanford won 76–60, Nnemkadi scoring thirty-nine points. Staley would coin a phrase she used often that offseason: "They didn't out-hustle us. They out-talented us."

The Gamecocks finished 25-10 with a Sweet 16 berth and a winning record in the SEC. So many steps had been taken.

"There's nothing that we can be mad about," Sutton said. "Stanford's a really good team."

The seniors had given so much to establish a legacy, but one that would die without being carried forward by the next team. That was the hardest part: the Gamecocks would be extremely young the next year and would lose some of their biggest pieces.

But as would become a cycle, talent replaced talent. The rocket ship was launched. USC lost fifty-eight games over Staley's first four seasons.

The Gamecocks would only lose twenty-two over the next five.

"I think the cupboards aren't bare," Staley said. "But certainly to fill the voids of our seniors departing will be huge. Hopefully we'll find ourselves back here."

8

TOPPLED

Assistant coaches seethed. Fans booed. Players were stunned and disbelieving.

It was one thing to lose.

It was another to have it stolen from them.

Dawn Staley took the high road after Tennessee beat South Carolina 76–74, ending two thirty-game winning streaks (against SEC competition and SEC home games). She could have screamed, threatened or declared that the controversial call that decided the game would be reviewed (athletics director Ray Tanner did send the call into the conference office afterward), but what good would it do?

The result wouldn't change. The Gamecocks lost. Her message to her team was the same as the officials had for USC.

Deal with it.

"I saw what everybody else saw," Staley said.

Look, the Gamecocks didn't play nearly to their capability. A tightly called game put A'ja Wilson, Alaina Coates, Allisha Gray and Tyasha Harris in foul trouble, including a technical on Wilson for a bad word she said—not toward an official, just in the heat of the moment after another foul. Tennessee, a reeling team that lost three of its first six SEC games, outscored USC by twelve points in the paint and went right at the Gamecocks in the fourth quarter, building a 69–60 lead with just over four minutes to play.

But USC wouldn't go away, Bianca Cuevas-Moore once again galloping to the rescue. Her three-pointer tied the game with fifteen seconds to go, and Colonial Life Arena could feel it. Another thirteen-thousand-plus crowd knew this was the time when their ladies would once again find a way to win and keep their status as the queens of the SEC fully intact.

The Lady Vols' Jaime Nared, their top free-throw shooter, was going to have the ball. The Gamecocks knew not to foul—try to get the ball up top, and if she drives, stand in front of her with arms up and don't move. Let the contact be called—with a good chance it will go against Tennessee.

Harris, the freshman, was on Nared as she drove from the top. Coming right, Harris side-stepped as Nared had her forearm out. As Nared came to the right, her left foot bumped Harris's foot as Harris was standing with arms stretched out. Nared tumbled to the floor as the whistle blew.

Harris jumped up and down, her hands whirling in the signal for traveling. That was player-induced contact from the offensive side. It was either an offensive foul or a travel. It was USC ball with less than ten seconds—plenty of time to get down court and get off a shot to win. If not, overtime.

Her glee lasted a split second. The referee signaled block.

Block?

"I tripped on her foot, so…there's not much I could have done," Nared said, smiling. "I tripped, I'm a little clumsy."

Gray and Wilson had both hands cupped over their mouths. Coates glared disgustedly at the official. Cuevas-Moore had her hands spread wide, incredulous. Harris jumped again, this time in anger.

Nared's two free throws were the difference. The Lady Vols won.

Which, Staley said, is fine if you want to label it that way. To her team, she said it was a defeat, and a game at Kentucky was on deck.

What do you plan on doing about it?

"We really can't go off of the officiating," Wilson said. "Just got to go and keep doing us."

They responded, as they were willing and able to do. They beat Kentucky on the road to stop the losing streak at one game, then mauled Arkansas and Auburn. Playing No. 1 Connecticut on the road, when the Huskies were bidding for their 100th straight win, was competitive for the first eighteen minutes, but a rash of turnovers gave UConn a halftime lead. The result, a 66–55 loss, was expected. As good as USC had become, UConn was on another level. The Huskies' eleven national championships sometimes made a mockery of the NCAA tournament, since it was becoming more about who would have the honor of finishing second rather than first.

Yet the rise of social media, hot takes and the immediate criticism made it seem as if the Gamecocks had no business losing that game. Staley, no stranger to Twitter, saw all of it.

"We do got a lot of coaches out there that want to coach our basketball team," she zinged. "But you can't just coach on game days. Got to get in here, got to coach on waking up, losing to a team and then getting them back, psychologically. Be fans, don't be coaches, because there's a lot that goes into coaching. It's just not Xs and Os."

It had been like this for three straight years. The Gamecocks wanted to play UConn, to see if they could be the team that would knock the Huskies off their pedestal, and it hadn't yet happened. It's not to say USC wasn't an extremely talented team, but UConn was UConn. They don't lose because… because…well, because nobody can beat them.

Fans still thought USC would, though, even in circumstances like being in Gampel Pavilion when the Huskies had won ninety-nine straight. That game was close, but UConn, as it always did, took one opponent mistake and made it hurt.

"Win or lose, that game really doesn't have any bearings on us and our goals that we need. So we get a chance to get back out there and play in one of the toughest leagues in the country," Staley said. "I know a lot of people want us to be that finished product now. We're just trying to mesh it all together."

Against the Huskies, Wilson and Coates were as strong as ever, but the guards had suffered. Harris, supposed to direct much more than score, often had no passing lanes and had no choice but to shoot, but she couldn't convert, mustering seven points on eleven attempts. Cuevas-Moore was four for eight for eleven points but didn't get a lot of looks against UConn's defense.

The concern was Davis, who had a string of poor shooting games coming in. She was never going to stop shooting—and there's a lot of logic in that, since a slump can't be broken if a player doesn't try—but not much was going in. Davis had three points at UConn and was one-of-ten from the field.

As for Staley's seeming inability to "win the big one," as a handful of fans complained, that would take care of itself.

After another hiccup, as it turned out.

The Gamecocks returned home and blistered Vanderbilt before heading back out on the road. Missouri, a rising team due to the homegrown talent of guard Sophie Cunningham, awaited. The Tennessee loss and Mississippi State's unbeaten response since losing to USC had the Gamecocks tied for first place, but they held the tiebreaker and would still win the title and No. 1 seed if the teams remained even at the end of the year.

USC's confidence wasn't shaken at all. Tennessee was a bad call, and UConn was UConn at its place on the verge of history. But the trip to the other Columbia would be the season's turning point.

Missouri won 62–60. The Gamecocks let Cunningham knife their defense for twenty-six points, including the final six. Coates, hampered by an ankle injury that seemed a minor twinge at the time, fouled out with two points and three rebounds. Deprived of their one-two punch in the paint, USC got the ball to Wilson for twenty-three points, but nobody else could get cooking.

USC, just as it did against Syracuse in that bitter Sweet 16 loss, was settling for three-pointers and not making them (a horrid three of eighteen). Davis, after sparkling so wonderfully at times through the year, was a miserable two of eleven from the field (zero of six from three) for six points. Gray wasn't much better, although she scored thirteen. Cuevas-Moore and Harris were a combined one of ten from the field.

Davis's foul/turnover after she was whistled for charging with twenty-three seconds in a tie game cleared Cunningham for the game-winning layup. It was the final lousy play in a lousy loss produced by the entire team. Nobody played to their full capability.

"When you leave people who think they can really shoot the ball open for as long and for as much as they were open…we bit the bullet and wanted to get one to fall. Sometimes, when you're trying to get one to fall, you lose sight of what is happening out there on the floor and who is having a great game, because A'ja Wilson had her way," Staley said. "You lose sight of that."

"Missouri was a good team that was well-motivated and played out of their minds that night. We missed some opportunities, for certain. That game meant a ton to them, similar to when South Carolina beat Tennessee up in Knoxville for the first time," radio voice Brad Muller said. "I wasn't worried about that game at the moment, but how the team would respond that late in the season. I remember getting on the plane a little angry over that one, because like most everybody, I'd gotten to used to them winning. They'd gone 16-0 the year before."

Nobody has a crystal ball or a time machine to go back and redo their mistakes. So the Gamecocks had no way of knowing what was ahead of them, especially with Coates hurt.

As for the mistakes they made, all they could do was try to repair them, one woman down or not. An inside-oriented team had lost a chunk of it at Missouri, and its guards weren't picking up the slack. Something had to change.

What was wrong with Davis? Why couldn't she snap herself out of this slump? She didn't have to score thirty-seven points per night like she did at Ohio State, but she couldn't keep throwing up these long misses that led to easy opponent runouts.

Gray was always there in the trenches, but there were times she needed to take her team under her wing and tell it what to do. So talented but so quiet, Gray had to deliver that kick to the rear end even if she required one herself.

The two point guards were starting to sputter, neither taking a definite hold of the job. That was another problem Staley had to try to conquer, with no easy solution. Pick one to take over, and the other's nose is out of joint at the most crucial time of the year. There wasn't anybody else left to play the spot without taking away from an established position.

Slipping from the top five in the polls and a world away from the team that was labeled the best in the country against Louisville, the Gamecocks were at a crossroads. They couldn't let this season also slip away. Couldn't.

"We're still playing well," Staley insisted. "Missouri played a great game. They got things to fall their way. We've responded well from losses we've taken this year, so I don't think there will be anything different."

Was confidence shaken? Had the armor been pierced?

"I thought we rebounded well from Connecticut, and we played well against Vandy. I felt we were in a good place, and I still think we are in a good place," Staley said. "Sometimes, it's just hard to continue to win, and [Missouri] has always been a hard place to win at."

MSU won that day, taking a one-game lead in the standings with two to play. The SEC championship hope was as good as dead. Coates was hurting, and her availability going forward was a question.

Staley thought throughout a long flight home. Her offense for years had run through the big girl, and now one big girl might be out for a while. One championship was pretty much lost, another couple were possible but the approach toward them may have to be revamped and no matter the circumstances, her team had lost three of its last seven games.

The Gamecocks couldn't know how desperate the situation seemed. And they wouldn't, not from her, her staff or anybody else. One, because that's not how Staley operates.

Two, and most importantly, a solution had appeared, out of necessity. And it could work.

Texas A&M waited in Columbia. Staley didn't talk about the loss, only the future, prefacing that nothing is ever as bad as it may seem. Winning the SEC was still possible.

"We welcome the challenge of finishing our year strong," she said. "And you never know."

9

SOARING

The hardest part of success is sustaining it. How many times had teams captured lightning in a bottle for one glorious season, or even one glorious decade, then discovered how hard it was to keep doing it as the slide seemed powerless to stop?

South Carolina was determined not to let that happen after the breakthrough of 2011–12.

"She came to me and she told me—'I need you to put yourself in a position to be more vocal, to learn and to evolve into that role,'" Aleighsa Welch said of Dawn Staley's offseason instructions that year.

It wasn't so much for that season—the Gamecocks had seniors Ieasia Walker and Ashley Bruner and a phenomenally talented freshman class, featuring Tiffany Mitchell, Khadijah Sessions and Asia Dozier. But Staley needed Welch to start taking more of an active role in commanding the team, the locker room, the practices.

Once Walker and Bruner were gone, it would be Welch's show.

It was an adjustment. If the motto read, "Lead, follow or get the hell out of the way," Welch had very much followed the latter the previous season. She didn't have to speak too loudly because others would do it for her, and it wasn't her place to start telling established players what was what.

"I needed guidance. I needed to be structured. When things were rocky, we respected how they want through the hardest times," Welch said. "But then they were gone. Coach was looking at me. Then my teammates voted me captain for three years."

As Staley had hoped, Welch's commitment was beginning to pay off with other South Carolina recruits. Dozier had played against Welch in state championship games while following her as South Carolina's Miss Basketball. Sessions was a Top 40 prospect who had scored over three thousand points in high school. Mitchell, a Staley superfan as a child, was North Carolina's Miss Basketball and also a top recruit.

Welch was instrumental in convincing all of them to stay local, not only by her success as a freshman—she led the Gamecocks in rebounding and was fourth in scoring—but also in how she talked to them on their visits to Columbia.

"I knew I wanted Asia to come. Tiffany was the same thing. When I was a recruit, I didn't always want to text or call because I was in high school, so with them, I waited until they came to campus," Welch said. "I was pretty direct, asking them, 'Do you want to be a part of something bigger?'"

With Staley and Welch double-teaming them with the same message— catch the elevator going up because it sure ain't coming back down—the Gamecocks began to nab the talent Staley coveted. USC had won a lot of games over the past two seasons by being tough, gritty and smart, and nobody would ever forget that hardened core of veterans who had led the way.

But now? In a game where, most often, the team with the most talent wins? USC had that talent.

"We're talented. I think we have some players that can create their own shots, that can wreak havoc on the defensive side," Staley said then. "But can they do it within our concepts, within what we're trying to do?"

"Last year, the Sweet 16 was great. But this year, our goal is the Final Four," Walker said, making no bones about where the Gamecocks expected to be even as practice was just beginning in October. "That's what we're working for."

The Gamecocks reeled off ten wins to start the season before they faced their first huge test. Stanford, which had ended its season in the Sweet 16 a year before, came to Columbia. The Cardinal had lost Nnemkadi Ogwumike but returned Chiney Ogwumike, and the team around her was ranked No. 1 in the country at the time.

Over eight thousand fans were at Colonial Life Arena to watch the Gamecocks stand toe-to-toe with Stanford. The suffocating defense USC had become known for held the Cardinal twenty-five points below their season average, and with 2:33 to go, a Sancheon White jumper had the Gamecocks leading 44–42.

But Ogwumike—it's always an Ogwumike—was fouled by Bruner on a made shot and converted the ensuing free throw, giving Stanford a one-point lead. Welch missed a shot, and White rebounded; Mitchell missed a shot, but Bruner stole the ball as Mikaela Ruef began to start a Stanford possession.

Welch was fouled with 1:14 to go, USC down one. She missed the first. (The Gamecocks were the country's worst team from the line the year before, despite their success. In 2012–13, they improved from dead last to next-to-last, converting a nearly unwatchable 56.4 percent of their free throws.)

Welch made the second to tie the game, but Ruef drained a jumper for a two-point lead. USC couldn't get enough offense in the final minute as Stanford pulled away, 53–49.

"We knew what it would come down to," Staley said. "Our ability to 'get buckets,' as we called them, and we fell short. We just couldn't put it in."

The Gamecocks lost their next two games against ranked opponents as well, by twenty to Tennessee and two to Georgia, before topping fifth-ranked Kentucky. That was in the midst of a six-game winning streak until a loss to Texas A&M—with the winning bucket courtesy of former USC star Kelsey Bone—snapped it.

USC wouldn't lose another home SEC game for four years.

The season ended in disappointment, although USC won another twenty-five games, with two fewer losses than the previous year. The Gamecocks also won eleven SEC games, a one-game improvement, but a 5-5 record in their final ten contests, and a Round of 32 exit to Kansas that was played in snowy Boulder, Colorado, dampened enthusiasm.

Staley turned down interest from Ohio State after that year, athletics director Ray Tanner proactively extending her contract after OSU contacted him for permission to speak to Staley. Staley thanked her boss and said she was looking forward to continuing to build and removing that season's disappointing finish.

As it turned out, though, that season was the aberration, the one bruise on an otherwise flawless apple. In 2013–14, the Gamecocks would start a run of never finishing less than the Sweet 16 and anywhere other than first in the SEC. They did it by continuing to hoard talent, local and otherwise, and taking a page from the book that Stanford used to beat them the last two seasons.

When in doubt, get the ball to the big girl.

ALAINA COATES HAD ALWAYS been the biggest kid on the court. At six feet, four inches when she entered USC, Coates was a hotly pursued prospect from Irmo who had dominated during her high school days. A McDonald's All-American center with great footwork, soft hands and an ability to score through contact in the paint, Coates wasn't just a terrific recruit—she was the future.

Yes, the Gamecocks had other pieces over the next four years, but as soon as Coates inked her letter-of-intent, USC went from a strong, solid tournament team to elite.

"She's done quite well, and I don't think we've had a player as strong as she is, physically," Staley said on the first day of practice for the 2013–14 season. "We have to tap into that—it's something we haven't had since I've been here."

That wasn't a shot at the ones who came before, the Stephenses and Bruners who had done yeoman's work on the block despite being undersized. Stephens, especially, made up for her lack of height with an iron will, refusing to be moved aside by bigger players.

But now USC had its own Ogwumike, if you will. Coates was going to play, and play a lot, and with Welch, Mitchell, Ibiam and Dozier around her, plus Sessions taking the point guard spot that Walker had helmed, the Gamecocks were exceedingly dangerous in every game they played.

They again won their first ten games, some on the road, but none over anybody of note. Then came the rematch with the Tar Heels in Myrtle Beach, after North Carolina had reloaded its roster with the best recruiting class in the country.

USC was drilled 74–66, unable to contain Stephanie Mavunga and Columbia's own Xylina McDaniel, the daughter of former NBA bruiser Xavier McDaniel. The Tar Heels also threw a couple of players at the Gamecocks that they'd see again, in different uniforms: Diamond DeShields and Allisha Gray.

The Gamecocks rebounded to win their next seven, losing a two-point overtime game at Texas A&M but winning their next ten to clinch their first SEC regular-season championship and top seed in the SEC tournament. Mitchell was SEC Player of the Year, Coates was SEC Freshman and Sixth Woman of the Year and Staley was SEC Coach of the Year.

"I thought we were close, but I didn't know if we were going to be that good, because we hadn't done it yet. I thought we were one of the top four teams in the league, but sometimes, it's not the top four that finishes in the top four," Brad Muller said. "The freshmen the year before took off as sophomores and that team just melded together. We've checked off another box that Dawn said we were going to do, and now, how could you deny anything else she said?"

But they again couldn't solve the Tar Heels in the NCAA tournament, falling 65–58 in the Sweet 16 at Stanford. DeShields and Gray helped end USC's season, and the Tar Heels were responsible for two of the Gamecocks' five losses that season.

"We had a tremendous amount of talent. We just didn't quite have enough," Welch said. "But we had our sights on what we could see. We had the talent in-house. Tiffany had taken that leap she took in that offseason to become our go-to player, winning Player of the Year, and the personal growth that everybody had, we knew what we were capable of."

That "didn't quite have enough" talent that Welch referenced?

It was on the way.

IT'S THE TITLE TRACK off Steely Dan's bestselling album. Roscoe Wilson, a six-foot, eight-inch behemoth who once pulled thirty-five rebounds in a game, used to listen to it during his lengthy overseas professional playing career.

"I just liked the song," Wilson said. "Not a lot of message in it, but it got me settled down, got me thinking, got me focused the night before the game and on the day of the game. It's easily spelled, so I said, 'If I ever have a daughter, I'm going to name her A'ja.'"

In a world where the most popular celebrities go by just one name (Beyoncé, Madonna) or are known by just one name (Elvis, Angelina), college coaches were beating a path to Columbia from 2012 to 2014. Their target was the simple, three-letter two-syllable name who had become the top recruit in the country for the class of 2014.

A'ja.

Six feet, five inches. Dominant in the post. She ran with gazelle-like strides down court and could not only play defense but also excelled at it. The small gym at Heathwood Hall Episcopal School in Columbia's south end, a few bounce passes away from where Williams-Brice Stadium marked the entrance to Gamecock Nation, was packed every night the Lady Highlanders played.

A'ja Wilson had always been a natural athlete, but as Roscoe saw his little girl growing, he knew she'd be a natural on the basketball floor. He asked her if she wanted to, warning her that if she said yes, there would be no turning back. They were going to go all-out to make her into the best player anybody had ever seen.

"She matured a lot quicker in emotion than a lot of kids did," Roscoe said.

Wilson had to, when her dad made her wear a vest lined with weights and shoot layups, first left hand, then right. A natural southpaw, she learned to dribble and finish from the right. East–west, not north–south, became a staple of her game; aggression toward the rim to avoid that five-second call became another.

She never quit, somehow finding time to also be a teenage girl and keep her high-voltage smile intact. All of the work paid off, as she became the best player in the country, a gold medalist at age sixteen and the future of the four schools she named as finalists: North Carolina, Tennessee, Connecticut and South Carolina.

Staley made sure the Gamecocks would be one of those four and did everything else she could to let Wilson know USC was going to be right there with those other three programs. Maybe the historical aspect wasn't there, but the message she preached to Welch and Mitchell and Coates was the same as she did to Wilson—come make history.

The neon-green T-shirts reading "There's no place like home," created for the Gamecocks' Colonial Life Arena attendees, certainly helped Staley and her staff stand out in a crowd…such as a high school game during an open recruiting period. During Heathwood's march to the state championship in Wilson's senior year, the four sections of bleachers on one side of the gym had notable company on every front step: the Gamecocks' staff, UConn's staff, UNC's staff and Tennessee's staff.

The hectic mania of her recruitment stretched until mid-April 2014, when Wilson sat in the gym where she had become this desired commodity, an arena that still has a wall-covering banner of her in her Heathwood uniform, ever-present pearl necklace matching her smile, adorning one side. She didn't milk the ceremony as she hadn't her recruitment, playing a game with hats on the table or saying one school, then saying another.

A TV announcer asked her where she was going. Four coaching staffs held their collective breath. The scream Staley and her assistants let out five seconds later could be heard in the middle of the Atlantic Ocean.

"There's just no place like home, there really isn't," Wilson said, donning her own neon T-shirt. "Coach Staley's really starting on something great, and I would love to be a part of it."

Wilson's pledge gave Staley the No. 2 class in the country, which also featured Bianca Cuevas-Moore and Doniyah Cliney. Joining a team that won twenty-nine games a year before and garnered an SEC championship, Wilson's decision immediately made the Gamecocks one of the teams to beat in 2014–15.

"We got to get A'ja Wilson. We got to get A'ja Wilson," Welch said. "Once that season ended and we got that class, my whole mood changed. We were now a team that you were going to have to circle, we went to always having the most talented fighters to having some of the best talent in the country on the court."

The Gamecocks debuted at No. 2 in the national polls and quickly rose to No. 1 when Connecticut lost, staying there as they won all of their first twenty-two games. Wilson paved the way in wins over Syracuse and Duke, immediately making the Gamecocks too much to handle for nearly all of their opponents.

They were too talented, too big, too fast. One solution would be found on how to stop them, and another would immediately rise to replace it. They were topped by UConn in Storrs but responded by clinching their second straight regular-season SEC championship, a final-game loss to Kentucky denying them a perfect 16-0 league record. Yet they went into the SEC tournament looking to avenge it and did, winning their first tournament championship with a 62–46 whipping of Tennessee.

"A team with that much talent has to check its ego. Everybody had to check their ego at the door," Welch said. "I played with so many players who were willing to come off the bench….A'ja and Alaina were OK with their roles. Tiffany was OK with not getting as many shots. I thought, 'If we can keep this same attitude, it's going to take it further than we ever dreamed.'"

Wilson was SEC Freshman of the Year; Mitchell repeated as SEC Player of the Year. A No. 1 seed in the NCAA tournament allowed them to stay at home for the first two games, where they easily dispatched Savannah State and Syracuse before heading up the road to Greensboro, North Carolina, where they would face nemesis and home-state favorite UNC.

DeShields had left, transferring to Tennessee, but the Tar Heels were still plenty dangerous. USC came in with the mindset of taking that next step, one that had thus far been denied them.

"We talked about not repeating history, them beating us again," Mitchell said. "It was about making history and getting to the eight."

Down 63–60 with 2:45 to play, the Gamecocks had any one of a plethora of stars to turn to. Welch, Wilson, Coates, Mitchell, Sessions, Dozier—any could get that crucial bucket and turn that game into a win.

Instead, it was a sparsely thought-of junior college project from Chester, South Carolina, who stole the show.

Just as she had in the win against Duke, when she played less than seven seconds but came up with a crucial steal to set up Wilson's game-winning tip-in, Olivia Gaines made an impact in her brief minutes. A defensive stopper, Gaines rebounded her own missed free throw and kicked the ball to Sessions, who wanted a chance to redeem herself after an awful Sweet 16 game against the Tar Heels a year before.

Instead, she saw Gaines, who had slipped to the corner without a defender, and passed her the ball. Gaines shot the ugliest three-pointer in basketball history, one that was heading right for the wedge joining the glass to the rim. The no-chance shot hit glass, hit rim, bounced up…and beautifully slid through the net.

"I heard coach tell me just to be ready, and I was ready," Gaines said. "I spotted up and knocked it down."

Coates made two free throws for a 65–63 USC lead, and there was no question who Staley would go to next. Following a timeout after UNC's tying layup, Staley drew up a play for "Superwoman."

Talk about the best players in South Carolina history, and it's debatable. There are several answers, and not one of them is wrong.

But when talking about the most talented players, the ones who could do everything with a basketball short of making it talk, it's a short list. Mitchell is at the very top of it.

"Any time that the game is on the line, Tiffany Mitchell will be around the ball," Staley said.

Mitchell bounced into the lane as the defense fell away, Welch screening a defender away from her teammate. Mitchell put in an unmolested layup with 4.2 seconds to play, Jaime Cherry's three-point attempt hit high off the glass and away and the Gamecocks were in the Elite Eight.

They'd planned to be there all year. "Final Four" had been said so often that it became an expectation, and it would be a disappointment if the Gamecocks didn't get there. Coming into that game, after having already done so much, USC was under pressure—but it also knew it had the team to overcome it.

Like UNC, Florida State took an early lead before Staley's adjustment proved prophetic. Cuevas-Moore came off the bench and energized the Gamecocks, who reset their offense and pulled back from a first-half deficit. Mitchell handled the ball on three straight possessions, all the same play, scoring and continuing to score. Her three-pointer put USC up five, Dozier took it home from the free-throw line and Sessions ended it with another firework.

The Seminoles' only chance to tie was to hit a three-pointer while being fouled and make the free throw. Sessions, guarding the dribble, never let it get remotely close to that.

She poked the ball loose and laid it in as the glass turned red on an 80–74 win. Staley called her assistants to her at the scorer's table for a group hug as her joyous team completed a forecasted mission.

South Carolina was going to the Final Four.

WELCH BROODED OVER IT, realizing how much the game meant and how badly she wanted it. USC was this close to a national championship, and if they could just get past Notre Dame, they'd be in that final game she'd dreamed about for so long.

"My biggest thing was give it all you got," she said. "I didn't want to regret anything."

It was right there to be had. USC had a one-point lead with less than a minute to go, and Welch came off the screen, wide open for a mid-range jumper. But it rimmed out, Irish star Jewell Loyd grabbed the rebound and was already in motion.

The agony of it was Notre Dame couldn't have done it again if locked in the gym all night. The Gamecocks had that final play pegged and were still undone.

Loyd's jumper was tipped by Wilson, an air ball that fell right to Madison Cable, who was cutting underneath the basket. She grabbed it and without looking—all the Gamecocks still swear Cable never even eyed the basket before she put it back up—it went in.

"There's never been a time other than that time that I wish a ball would have hit the rim," Welch said. "That ball hits any part of the rim, we're not talking about this. I thought the whole summer, 'I was there. Just let me get a fingertip on it…' I missed it by maybe a centimeter. And it went in."

Notre Dame led 66–65. The Gamecocks had plenty of time and weapons to defeat it, but Mitchell was covered. She had no open look, no way to pass, and her desperation three-pointer was well off the mark.

It was over.

"I've seen clips, maybe half the game. It's still hard to swallow. Maybe when I'm thirty, but I'm only twenty-two and it's still fresh," Mitchell said. "We were a bucket away from playing for a championship."

Welch crouched at midcourt, unable to stop the tears that burst from her eyes. "Muffin" left school as one of the Gamecocks' all-time finest, but she still remembers the one she didn't get over so many she did.

"There was nobody else I wanted to take the last shot," Welch said. "If it got up with a rebound, I was going to go for it and there was nobody who was going to keep me off the board.

"It took me a solid year to be able to watch it just because of how we lost. If I lose, I'd rather get blown out than to lose how we lost. The fact that it was done, my four years were over...that we had done something nobody expected was great, but I wanted that game back."

The Gamecocks had come so far only to be denied. It was the same story in 2015–16, when another magnificently talented team that went 16-0 in the SEC, with another regular-season championship and tournament title, was knocked out of the Sweet 16 by Syracuse.

It's such a small window to get through. Even though the Gamecocks had only been to one Final Four, the last two postseasons made USC and Staley wonder if they'd lost their best chance. Staley knew better than anybody that a certain group of players, a collection of chemistry like USC had, is very special and it's not just minted and replicated.

Would they ever get another shot?

Right: Dawn Staley coaching her team to another win over Kentucky among four straight SEC regular-season championships.

Middle: The 2015 Final Four didn't go the Gamecocks' way, as Notre Dame coach Muffet McGraw consoles Aleighsa Welch and Elem Ibiam.

Bottom: Kaela Davis exults as the Gamecocks close out Arizona State and head to the Sweet 16.

Left: Aleighsa Welch was Dawn Staley's first homegrown recruit and finished her career with four straight NCAA tournament appearances and a Final Four.

Right: The fifth time was the charm for Dawn Staley, who participated in her second championship game among five Final Fours and got that elusive title.

Alaina Coates was a vital part of the Gamecocks' rise to elite status. She won a conference championship in each of her four years.

La'Keisha Sutton, the captain of the Gamecocks' first NCAA tournament team under Dawn Staley.

Tiffany Mitchell, two-time SEC Player of the Year and a key cog of the Gamecocks' rise into a Final Four program.

A'ja Wilson slices through Mississippi State's defense in Dallas.

Top: A'ja Wilson and Alaina Coates, twin towers for three seasons.

Middle: Dawn Staley was never hesitant to play the transfer market. Allisha Gray, from North Carolina, was a vital part of the 2017 national championship team.

Below: Freshman Tyasha Harris took over as starting point guard during the Gamecocks' SEC schedule.

Bianca Cuevas-Moore, a savvy and speedy guard from the Bronx, was one of the numerous McDonald's All-Americans who pledged to Dawn Staley.

Kaela Davis transferred from Georgia Tech and immediately became a go-to scorer for the 2016–17 Gamecocks.

Left: A'ja Wilson soars for the ball against Mississippi State in the SEC tournament championship.

Right: A'ja Wilson knows she and her teammates are going to play for a national title after beating Stanford.

Alaina Coates's ankle gave out in the SEC tournament. She would not return from the injury.

Injured ankle and all, Alaina Coates (*right*) made it to the floor to celebrate USC's back-to-back-to-back SEC tournament championships.

Allisha Gray nabs a rebound against UNC–Asheville in the first round of the NCAA tournament.

Left: USC's coaching staff hugs just before the final horn sounds in the national championship game.

Middle: Dawn Staley thanks the thousands of fans who lined Main Street for the championship parade.

Bottom: The Gamecocks file through the crowd toward the statehouse steps as they're honored for their first national championship.

10

WE ARE THE CHAMPIONS...AGAIN

They staggered home from Missouri, one of their best players injured and out for who knew how long and their shot at a fourth straight SEC regular-season championship all but gone. Mississippi State, despite losing to South Carolina, was ahead one game in the standings with two to play, and while the Gamecocks still had a slim chance, the smart money said not to bet on it.

Dawn Staley was at a crossroads. The team could handle losing, although it had happened three times in the last seven games. She wasn't worried about that.

What she was most concerned over was Alaina Coates, who hurt her ankle at Missouri and might not be available going forward.

"We got to take the good with the bad, and sometimes the bad is losing one here or there," Staley said. "Not in control of our own destiny at this point when it comes to the regular-season championship, but just got to continue on our path of getting better, playing the perfect game and despite our loss, we're still playing well."

She didn't know if Coates would play the next game, at Texas A&M, but she had a sneaking suspicion that her center would do anything she had to do to play her Senior Day against Kentucky the game after. The problem was how the Gamecocks were going to go on the road to an arena where not many opponents win, where they'd never played particularly well, and reinvent their offense to cover the loss of their big girl.

"Dawn didn't bring it up. She's already in next-game mode, and that's something she stresses to the team," radio voice Brad Muller said. "The next day, I was still disappointed but knew there was still a lot in front of them. The only issue was they didn't play well at Missouri."

Staley didn't have a lot of options with an already-thin bench, but she had an idea. Bianca Cuevas-Moore had handled being bumped from the starting point guard spot well, the junior playing a crucial role off the bench and spelling Tyasha Harris when she needed a break.

What if both started?

The move made sense. Not many could keep up with the Gamecocks if they ran for forty minutes, and with Cuevas-Moore and Harris each taking the ball inside, not letting the defenses set up on the perimeter, they could either score at the rim or kick to Kaela Davis and Allisha Gray, who could drift to mid-range spots or to the three-point line. There was also A'ja Wilson, who was always waiting to score from the block or keep a possession alive with a tipped ball or rebound.

The Xs and Os plan was intact. Cuevas-Moore and Harris would each start and let A&M figure out how to guard them. Staley then switched to the second part of the plan: telling the Gamecocks not to worry about the standings and the SEC title. If it doesn't happen, it doesn't happen.

Mississippi State was playing at Kentucky, a win meaning the championship was theirs. USC tipped off an hour after the Bulldogs and Wildcats. The Gamecocks wouldn't scoreboard-watch anyway, but if they were being tempted to, the start times squelched the temptation.

The experiment was working. Cuevas-Moore and Harris were charging right through the Aggies' scattered defense and taking high-percentage shots, something nobody in a USC uniform did at Missouri. The Gamecocks would end with fifty-four of their eighty points in the paint; Cuevas-Moore tied for the team high with thirty-six minutes and scored sixteen points.

Wilson had twenty-one along with fifteen rebounds, three blocks and three steals, while Mikiah "Kiki" Herbert Harrigan scored thirteen. The "speed" lineup resulted in a whopping thirteen steals among fifteen forced turnovers, and the Gamecocks put it away with a 19–6 burst in the third quarter.

They were justifiably proud of what they'd done, walking into a hostile gym and winning to get themselves off a loss. Then they fired up their phones or heard the news already circulating: Kentucky, their bad-blood conference rival, had done them a favor and beaten Mississippi State. USC and the Bulldogs were tied for first place with one game to go.

Against the odds, when they were at their lowest, USC was still right there in contention for the SEC championship. All the Gamecocks had to do was beat Kentucky at home on Senior Day, and they'd be champions for the fourth straight year. Mississippi State could beat Tennessee on its Senior Day and also be named champion. Ties are only broken for tournament seeding, and if two, three or four teams are tied for first at the end of the year, all are named champion—but the Gamecocks would remain the No. 1 seed for the SEC tournament due to beating Mississippi State during the regular season.

The term "split title" isn't very accurate since it's not like the SEC would cut the trophy in halves, thirds or quarters in the event of a tie. Each team would get a trophy and be able to order a ring and hang a banner. None would say "co-champions," either—they'd just read "champions." That was the case when the Gamecocks and Tennessee tied for first to end the 2014–15 season, but USC still had the tiebreaker and No. 1 seed for the SEC tournament.

Of course the Gamecocks would prefer it be an undisputed championship, but they couldn't control that. All they knew was that if they beat Kentucky, they'd be one of two teams in SEC history to win the regular-season championship at least four years in a row (the Lady Vols hold the record with seven straight).

The preparation was the same as it was for Texas A&M, although USC now had a hole card. The two–point guard lineup could work, but Staley was confident—and correct—that Coates was not going to miss her Senior Day. The senior would wind up starting and playing twenty-seven minutes.

As for the Wildcats, which USC had beaten five straight times following the one blemish on a 15-1 SEC record in 2014–15, the Gamecocks owed them. Had they not beaten Mississippi State, USC wouldn't have a title shot.

They'd thank them.

After.

"I was a Big Blue Nation fan. But, I think it's back on," Staley said. "The rival cap is back on."

USC led by fourteen points in the fourth quarter as a celebratory Colonial Life Arena took on a party atmosphere. Wilson was putting the final touches on her second straight SEC Player of the Year campaign with twenty-five points and ten rebounds, while Davis had twenty and Gray seventeen. Coates and Harris had thirteen points each.

But Kentucky kept coming. Taylor Murray had taken the slack left by star Makayla Epps (held to ten points) by scoring twenty-nine. The Wildcats crept within six points with 4:48 to go before Gray rebounded her own miss to score and Wilson put back Doniyah Cliney's missed layup.

The Gamecocks cruised home from there, finishing a coronation of domination. It got even sweeter a few hours later—Tennessee had beaten Mississippi State.

USC was SEC champion. Undisputed.

One more time.

"It's been a bumpy road this year....It hasn't been easy," Wilson said. "It's never been easy."

And the one trophy was just a piece of what they hoped to accomplish. The Gamecocks would be the No. 1 seed in the SEC tournament, which would be played just up the road at Greenville's Bon Secours Wellness Arena. Winners of the last two tournaments, the Gamecocks didn't want to disappoint their home fans who had snapped up tickets the moment the site was announced.

"I don't think our players are really keying on where we are as a seed," Staley said. "Those things are out of our control as well. What we are in control of is playing each game and executing and doing the things that got us here."

THE GAMECOCKS HAD A couple of extra days to rest, since they wouldn't have to play in the tournament until Friday. All attention immediately turned to Coates's ankle.

She'd played and played well against Kentucky, but the ankle was still aggravating her. Nobody knew if it would hold up in three games in the tournament, or if USC could even get to three games in the tournament. Set up against Georgia for the third time of the season—the Gamecocks won each, but the first was by a mere three points and both had been meat-grinding physical affairs—Staley was faced with another gamble.

The smaller lineup had worked against A&M, and she was confident it could work again. She really wanted Coates on the floor, but if resting her could save her for the NCAA tournament, well...

It's not like she was discounting the SEC tournament, but if she had to pick one for Coates to play in, it would be the NCAA.

Coates would sit the first game of the tournament, and if she could play going forward, she'd play going forward. But for now, it was the same as the A&M game.

Go to work, ladies.

Herbert Harrigan was a surprise starter, but Cuevas-Moore quickly came in, restoring the quickness the Gamecocks had come to depend on. The rest was a controlled pasting of the Bulldogs, 72–48, and more confidence going into the semifinals.

"We've been practicing with the small lineup a lot, even before Alaina got hurt. Once A'ja got hurt, we played the smaller lineup because we got some good looks out of it," Staley said. "It's the mark of a really good team that's able to take advantage of those adverse moments."

The Gamecocks stayed off the three-point line and worked the paint, Wilson finishing with eighteen points and seven blocked shots. Gray added seventeen.

USC's defense crunched Georgia into a trap featuring eighteen turnovers and a miserable 28.1 shooting percentage as icy as Greenville's hockey-arena environment. Staley was again questioned about Coates before the next game—which would again feature Kentucky—but she didn't know anything other than what she knew before Georgia. It was a wait-and-see.

But USC was prepared to go without her, if that's what it had to do.

"It's something we've been working on, to allow our players to play off what they naturally do," Staley said. "Allisha is able to go downhill a little bit on the floor. Kaela is getting used to putting that ball on the floor, getting to the basket, which I like, being very, very aggressive. All of them."

AFTER THE GAME, COATES said she felt fine. There were no tears, grimaces or downcast expressions.

"We're just trying to do everything that we can to get me healed up for NCAA," she said after the Gamecocks again took out Kentucky, 89–77, advancing to their third straight SEC tournament championship game. "I'm not going to play anymore for the tournament for the simple fact that I've got to think about the future and the NCAA tournament. It was a freak accident type of thing."

Coates only played four minutes, Herbert Harrigan again starting and playing well alongside Wilson. The freshman had seventeen points and two blocked shots, while Wilson was Wilson with twenty-six points. Davis (seventeen) and Cuevas-Moore (thirteen) rounded out another complete effort, the Gamecocks' bench out-scoring Kentucky 18–0.

But everyone was thinking about Coates, who was only used a couple of times but the last just enough to get her re-injured. She came in for Herbert Harrigan in the final two minutes of the third quarter, the Gamecocks needing to reestablish themselves as a thirteen-point lead was sliced to six.

The Wildcats reeled off four quick points around a Wilson turnover, and then it happened. Coates had the ball under the basket and spun around to establish position when her ankle gave way. She hit the deck and was immediately pounding the floor in agonized frustration.

From her reaction after the game, it was just a scare. As Staley said, any time a player had been virtually injury-free her entire career and then got hurt, feeling any twinge or tweak can often take the psychological effect of making the player feel more hurt than they actually are. Coates was perfectly fine after the game but would miss the championship contest, which like the year before, would be against Mississippi State.

But she'd be fine going forward. No question.

MISSISSIPPI STATE SEETHED BECAUSE it had the SEC regular-season championship right in its hands and let it slip away. The Bulldogs were making a habit, and not a pleasant one, of winning more games than ever, setting numerous school records but coming *this* close to glory before falling short.

"I walked out of that building with a bunch of confidence," coach Vic Schaefer said of the regular-season matchup, a 64–61 USC win in Columbia. "I mean, we missed a layup with thirty-something seconds left to go up one. We've got the ball, seventeen seconds. We've got an out-of-bounds play. We didn't walk out hanging our head, 'We just lost the championship.' We walked out of there going, 'We're pretty good.' They're still going to have to play a bunch of games. See how the chips fall. They fell and gave us our chance."

But the Bulldogs didn't grab it, losing to Kentucky and Tennessee as the Gamecocks once again sprinted to the finish line. They were looking to get that one back by dethroning the Gamecocks on what amounted to their home floor.

Ahead 45–40 with a period to go, the Bulldogs could feel it. Their own mammoth center, six-foot, seven-inch Teaira McCowan, was limiting Wilson inside, and there was nobody else to throw the ball to in the paint with Coates sidelined. Twenty-three points from Davis were keeping the Gamecocks in it, but they needed to make a move.

Wilson did.

"Just during the timeout, coach pointed at her chest, it means heart," said Wilson, who scored seven of her fifteen points, grabbed eight of her nine rebounds and blocked a shot in the fourth quarter. "That's what it comes down to. In a championship game, it comes down to who wants it more."

Wilson converted four shots from the line to settle an 8–0 lead-restoring run, and the Gamecocks' defense again began slowly choking the life out of Mississippi State. Harris nearly threw a possession away with a risky pass inside, but Cliney saved it and gave it right back. Harris had to do something with the shot clock about to expire so she threw it up there—the crowd knew it was good as soon as it left her hand.

Wilson was named tournament MVP after the 59–49 win, while Davis also made the all-tournament team. The Gamecocks limited MSU to four points in the fourth as they took their third consecutive tournament crown and clinched yet another No. 1 seed in the NCAA tournament.

Everything was clicking. USC had won two championships in a week and did it mostly without one of their vital players. They would be a formidable opponent in the NCAA tournament.

As long as nothing else happened.

11

WOMAN DOWN

Where the hell is Stockton, California?

Right in the middle of the state, home to the University of the Pacific, Stockton is easily reachable by a few major airports. An hour south from Sacramento and eighty minutes east of San Francisco, the city of 315,000 boasts two professional teams, although both are in the minor leagues: hockey's Stockton Heat and baseball's Stockton Ports.

Great.

But where the hell is Stockton, California?

It's where South Carolina would be playing its Sweet 16 and Elite Eight games—if it got that far—in the 2017 NCAA tournament. The Gamecocks' reward for winning twenty-seven games, beating many of the nation's top teams on the road, claiming a fourth straight SEC regular-season championship and third straight SEC tournament and earning a No. 1 seed in the NCAA tournament was being sent across the country, 2,600 miles away from the most loyal fan base in America.

"I don't know what more we can do. We won our conference tournament to play closer," grumbled Dawn Staley. "I'm very disappointed. We're always the team, three out of the four years that we've been number-one seeds, that has to fly over two or three time zones. I'm not saying it's not fair, but they got to figure out a different way, especially when we played our way into that number-three number-one seed."

The Gamecocks ran into the same problem they did in 2016, when they were sent to Sioux Falls, South Dakota, instead of a closer, warmer climate.

The NCAA women's tournament regional sites, predetermined years in advance, had chosen regionals somewhat around the country's four main areas (North, South, East, West).

After advancing to the Final Four out of Greensboro, North Carolina, in 2015, the Gamecocks were hoping to be sent to Lexington, Kentucky, from 2016 to 2018. Rupp Arena would host each of the three years, and it was closest to Columbia, an easy six-and-a-half- to seven-hour drive from USC. The other 2016 regionals were in Bridgeport, Connecticut (where Connecticut would obviously be the top seed), Dallas and Sioux Falls.

Baylor was sent to Dallas, a simple trot up the road from its campus in Waco, Texas. That left Notre Dame and USC fighting for the Kentucky spot.

Notre Dame won. Hey, these things happen. But the NCAA's logic for the decision was infuriating.

The NCAA ruled that when it comes to traveling to regional sites, a 350-mile radius was employed. If the regional site was within a 350-mile drive from campus, that school was sent to that regional.

South Bend, Indiana, was within that circle. Columbia was not. Therefore, by the NCAA's logic, Lexington was a flight from Kentucky.

Anybody who had cheered for the Gamecocks since 1992 knew that was hogwash. Fans routinely make the drive to Lexington every other year for football. It's not difficult. But the NCAA said that by its rules, it was a flight, and a flight is a flight.

Translation: you got to get on a plane anyway, so you might as well take a long flight. Which is why the Gamecocks were being sent to South Dakota in 2016 and Stockton in 2017.

Staley was put out because she felt the team with the higher seed should be given first preference, but the NCAA felt that the ranking of seeds didn't matter so much as the geography. In men's regionals, it wouldn't matter—fans will show up no matter who's playing there because it's a big-time event, either from the local community or team fans who make the trip.

In women's regionals, the NCAA needs fans willing to go support their team to fill those regional arenas. That's why UConn always has one close by its campus. If Notre Dame or USC was sent to Stockton, well, Lexington would probably be full of one fan base but Stockton wouldn't be. Six of one, half a dozen of the other.

The Gamecocks were frustrated and had little comfort for the future. The 2018 regional sites were Albany, Kansas City, Lexington and Spokane. If UConn, Notre Dame, Baylor and USC were again No. 1 seeds…

No use wondering what might happen or what could happen. Staley wrapped up the press conference and said that part of the equation was over. Stockton wouldn't matter if the Gamecocks didn't win their first two games.

And the next day, that journey had a six-foot, four-inch roadblock.

THE SIMPLE FOUR-PARAGRAPH PRESS release seemed as routine as announcing a new paint job on the stadium walls. "South Carolina senior center Alaina Coates will not participate in the 2017 NCAA tournament as she continues her recovery from an ankle injury, head coach Dawn Staley announced today," it said a day after the NCAA tournament selection.

"Oh, tough break," many said.

Then, "Wait, what?"

Alaina Coates is out? For good?

Staley had said Coates would be fine for the NCAA tournament. Many thought she might miss the first game because why risk it against a UNC–Asheville team the Gamecocks should easily handle without her?

But out for the whole tournament? No possibility of return?

No wrecking ball in the paint. No one-two punch in the lane that was a nightmare to scout. No surprise element for the opponents, as in, "I bet she *will* play and Dawn's just gaming us."

Worst of all, no culmination for Coates, who really wanted to add the biggest ring to fingers already brimming with them.

"That was always part of my plan, which is why I went to South Carolina," Coates said later. "For them to go out there and finish the season, especially without me…we just kept talking about going to get these rings."

The Gamecocks were down to ten eligible players. Two freshmen, Victoria Patrick and Araion Bradshaw, had scarce minutes throughout the year. Senior Tiffany Davis had a lot of experience but had, like Patrick and Bradshaw, been strictly a bench player.

The Gamecocks were basically going with seven players into the NCAA tournament. All would have to help fill the immense void left by Coates's injury.

"I think we all were hopeful that she would return, but I think it was a good test for us," Kaela Davis said. "And I think we kind of passed the test."

Staley had already adjusted how her team played mid-stream before, but that was supposed to be a stopgap, a Band-Aid on a problem that would soon go away.

This wasn't going away.

"We're different. Obviously we can play a little more free as far as space people out a little bit, create a little more driving lanes, not having the two bigs in there clogging up the paint," she said. "Where we probably suffer a little bit more is from a rebounding standpoint and defensively. Lay did a great job of protecting the paint for us. You can't just point to one thing because she's meant so much to us."

"She could get the rebound and get down the floor better than anybody in the country. She could run, she could score from anywhere in the paint," announcer Brad Muller said. "I was really disappointed I wouldn't get to see her play again, but in terms of being concerned with the team's chances, I was thinking they'd be OK as long as they didn't get into foul trouble. We had just won the SEC tournament without Alaina Coates so I knew they were at least used to her not being there. I felt we still were a Final Four team."

It was foreboding. Jumping miles ahead, most thought that any chance the Gamecocks had of beating UConn—because of course the Huskies would be in the Final Four and the championship game—just took a hard right turn. And before it even got that close, USC would have to beat a lot of other good teams.

Yeah, those others were good. But the Gamecocks were pretty good, too, even without Coates.

They had A'ja.

"The only part that we're really missing, and coach would always say this, is just the rebounding side of it. It's nothing really different from the past, it's just now we really have to execute it," Wilson said. "It is tough when you have a big part of your program not being able to participate in the way that she can. But we just have to fight through."

Wilson never showed the pressure she was feeling, but knew the burden of carrying her team forward was now on her shoulders.

Now, more than ever, was her time.

BIANCA CUEVAS-MOORE TWICE STRIPPED the ball from UNC–Asheville and finished each with layups, adding another layup after the Gamecocks got another steal and spied her streaking to the basket. The second-quarter burst erased a shuffling first quarter and keyed a 90–40 blowout of the Bulldogs in the first round of the NCAA tournament.

"Coach [Nikki McCray-Penson] said, 'I need you to get three steals in a row right here,' so I said, 'All right, I got you,'" Cuevas-Moore said. "I gave her a little bump, came out there, pressured the court and got that ball and scored."

Cuevas-Moore scored eighteen points with three assists in the return to the "speed" lineup, vital to the Gamecocks' chances of advancing with Coates sidelined. Allisha Gray had a double-double while leading USC with twenty-two points, and Wilson added eighteen points.

As Staley predicted, the new lineup opened the floor a bit more, allowing the Gamecocks to use their quickness five-on-five, instead of having a trailing center always on the lookout to get back and defend the paint. USC was like a swarm of spiders on UNC–Asheville, turning fourteen turnovers into twenty-three points.

"I just thought today, just going with a little more experience, and Bianca gave us an opportunity to get out and play a little bit quicker," Staley said. "You got two post players and you want to make sure that you balance them out and make sure that they stay out of foul trouble."

Mikiah "Kiki" Herbert Harrigan added fourteen points in twenty-five minutes, converting five of eight from the floor as her role increased. The Gamecocks easily advanced to the Round of 32, but that was expected, being a top seed versus a sixteenth seed.

Next up was Arizona State, a powerful team despite the eighth seed it received. The Sun Devils had been in the 2015 Sweet 16 with the Gamecocks in Greensboro, but the two teams never played after USC beat North Carolina and Florida State beat Arizona State.

This year, they had won some big games but were a mere 9-9 in the Pac-12, losing six of eight at one point. But the Sun Devils had little trouble with Michigan State in the first round and were confident they knew that as powerful as the Gamecocks could be, they weren't at their most powerful, even playing at home.

"This is the first time we've been fully healthy since November," coach Charli Turner Thorne said. "The advantage for us with our defense is when people haven't seen us play before, and I thought if we had played [Michigan State] a second time, they would have adjusted because Suzy Merchant is an amazing coach. But I think it is hard to play against us when you don't know how we play."

WHAT EXACTLY WAS GOING on here?

The Gamecocks were down at halftime, down the entire third quarter, but cut an eleven-point lead to two by the end of the period. They quickly tied the game in the fourth and from there built a ten-point lead with 5:51 to go. Davis swished a jumper for that lead, and Colonial Life Arena was celebrating. The last home game of the year would be yet another win; the Gamecocks were going to yet another Sweet 16 and were that much closer to Dallas and the Final Four.

The Sun Devils had other ideas.

Even after Wilson rejected Sophie Brunner twice in four seconds, Arizona State was in a zone. Wilson, after the two blocks, was called for her fourth foul on a turnover and had to take a seat; the Devils knew they'd never get a better chance.

Davis fouled Quinn Dornstauder after USC couldn't get a defensive rebound, but Dornstauder only made one free throw. Yet Kelsey Moos swiped the ball from Davis on the next possession and flipped it to Reili Richardson, who laid it in.

Seven-point lead.

Staley called timeout. Calm down, she told her team. Just do what got us here.

Doniyah Cliney had the ball taken from her by Dornstauder. Richardson bombed a three-pointer.

Four-point lead.

Wilson hurriedly reentered the game, 4:09 to go, as the crowd was getting antsy. No problem, though, just get the ball to Wilson, don't take any rushed, bad shots that she can't at least get a rebound off of.

Davis took a rushed, bad three that Brunner rebounded. Moos turned it into a jumper.

Two-point lead.

More disaster erupted as Gray missed a jumper and collapsed to the floor in agony. Nobody had touched her, either—she came down off the shot and her knee buckled. She had to be carried off the floor.

Gulp.

Cuevas-Moore entered. Sabrina Haines, who'd done nothing but camp on the three-point line all game, was open on the three-point line as USC collapsed on Dornstauder, who'd gotten the entry pass in the paint.

Kick-out, three-pointer.

Bang.

USC trailed by one with 124 seconds to play. The Gamecocks blew a ten-point lead in less than three minutes.

"I feel like we've been in that situation before, maybe not even in games but in practice," Wilson said. "We prepare very well for situations like that. I think we were prepared, and also in the Tennessee game I feel like that was another game where things kept changing, so I think we handled it really well."

That Tennessee game was on a lot of folks' minds. They couldn't end like this, could they? Not at home in the Round of 32.

Not another awful finish after a wonderful season.

Scrap any trick plays, any back-of-the-mind formations she saw one time and filed it away for just the right occasion. Staley ordered the best plan she could, and the only plan she could: get the ball to A'ja.

Now.

Wilson missed a jumper, but Brunner tanked a layup, seventy-one seconds to go.

That rail-thin girl with monstrous feet who worked with her father for countless hours, wearing a weighted vest and finishing layups, knew this was why she'd suffered through those sessions. She was going to have to go in the paint, where the bruisers were, and get it done.

Wilson drove in, Dornstauder standing there with arms up. There was contact, uncalled, as Wilson missed her first try.

Ponytail flying, Wilson elevated again for the rebound, laying in the putback. Gamecocks up one, forty-six seconds.

Staley subbed in Herbert Harrigan during the Sun Devils' timeout, needing height on the floor to get a rebound. It paid off, as the freshman grabbed a Brunner miss and passed to Harris, who was fouled by Haines.

As usual, the Gamecocks weren't a great free-throw team. They'd improved from the bottom of the barrel but still ranked 109th in the country in makes.

Harris bricked both shots. Brunner rebounded, and Arizona State called timeout.

Calling the game courtside, Muller felt confident, but there was the thought flashing through his mind—Syracuse.

"I thought the Arizona State game would depend on how it was called. I didn't think the crowd would let us lose at home," Muller said. "I thought it might come down to the last possession, and it did, but we had already overcome so much with losing Alaina, we weren't going to lose then. We had come too far."

Davis, still feeling awful about how she played against Missouri, was thinking of that and her decisions during the Devils' run. If there was any time to make up for it, it was now.

Davis stole the rock from Richardson and called timeout with eighteen seconds to play.

Everybody in that arena knew where that ball was going. Wilson received it and cradled it as Moos fouled her.

Big-time player. Big-time situation.

Big-time results.

Wilson coolly aced her two free throws, Brunner's desperation heave was well off the mark and the Gamecocks survived, 71–68. It wasn't pretty, wasn't confidence-inspiring, wasn't the way they drew it up.

But they won.

"I think throughout the game, you have to be positive. You can never put yourself in a position to feel down," said Davis, who scored twenty points with that crucial steal. "I think we just kept our heads down and didn't look at the score and just fought back."

Wilson, who finished with twenty-one and eleven rebounds, answered the same as she had throughout her career—"Call it pressure if you want, but I don't feel it. I'm here to do what I need to do."

"Our guards were doing a tremendous job of getting the ball in the basket, and that's what you need to win, so I really didn't care. I just wanted to hold up my end of the barrel, and I trust them and they trust me so I really wasn't worried," she said. "I just knew the ball was going to find who needs it."

12

WE HERE

T he beauty of the tournament is you can't help who you play. The brackets are seeded so the top four seeds have a great chance to get to the regional finals, but it usually doesn't work out that way.

So it was that the top three seeds in the Stockton Regional on Selection Sunday—No. 1 South Carolina, No. 2 Oregon State and No. 3 Florida State—advanced to Stockton, California, along with No. 12 seed Quinnipiac. Who?

Quinnipiac. KWIN-uh-pee-ack. The Bobcats. Located in Hamden, Connecticut. Proud alma mater of Murray Lender, who, as the *Washington Post* said, was probably the most important man in the modern history of bagels.

That was the Gamecocks' Sweet 16 opponent.

"I kind of know how to spell it…not really," forward A'ja Wilson joked. "I thought it was with an 'e' but it's not. They're a really good team, the Cinderella team, so-called, in our bracket. We really can't sleep on them, because we watched the Miami game, and the way that they came back, just the way that they played, it was great."

Wilson also warned that nobody ever wants to play a team with a story, and Quinnipiac definitely had that. The Bobcats went to Miami for the first two rounds and knocked off fifth-seed Marquette before stunning the fourth-seeded Hurricanes on their home court.

"I think we are really excited to be here, and just the opportunity at hand, you know, we're really grateful for it, and we're going to leave it all out on the floor," Quinnipiac's Morgan Manz gushed. "However long it takes, we'll hopefully get another upset."

Most looked at the matchup and snickered. The Gamecocks were served a delicious appetizer before the main course of Florida State/Oregon State, to be presented two days later.

But there was enough reason to be concerned. One, Allisha Gray was coming off a bad-looking knee injury against Arizona State. (She was fine, but USC couldn't afford to lose any more players.) Two, the Bobcats could shoot the three-pointer very well and they'd won twenty-nine games, just like USC had. Three, USC was still kicking rocks because it was playing in Stockton with no fans in sight, angry at the NCAA selection committee for exiling it across the country. Quinnipiac didn't care because it was still playing basketball, wherever that might be.

Four, the Gamecocks were the team with the history of failure in the Sweet 16, not the opponent. The memory of Syracuse in South Dakota a year before still burned.

But they'd had quite enough of that, thank you.

USC blistered the Bobcats 100–58, scoring the game's first sixteen points and never easing their feet off the gas pedal. Kaela Davis scored twenty-eight points, while Wilson had twenty-four and Gray nineteen.

The Gamecocks' defense was also sterling, denying Quinnipiac open looks from three and getting to every entry pass. The Bobcats had seventeen turnovers, and of their eighteen possessions in the first quarter, they had seven points.

"So our biggest thing was just making them put the ball on the floor, you know, and if we had to give up a two, we'd much rather give up a two rather than a three," Davis said. "We're going to play the way that we know how to play. No matter who is in front of us, we have to play hard. We have to come ready to play no matter who it is, as it was today."

Dawn Staley liked how her team handled the moment and the opponent and loved how the offense was becoming more and more relentless. Like she had planned at the start of the season, offense was what had been taught the most; it had to be relied on with Alaina Coates out of the picture.

"For the guards, like a Kaela Davis, she's getting to the basket a little bit more. Allisha Gray can play more downhill. Bianca Cuevas-Moore thrives off of the space that's left with the void of not having Alaina Coates in there," Staley said. "But we do, we feel from a rebounding and defensive standpoint, we feel her presence missed."

Next up was Florida State, a dangerous team featuring many of the same players the Gamecocks beat two years ago in Greensboro to get to the Final Four. ACC Player of the Year Shakayla Thomas, who Staley coveted for her already-bursting recruiting class of 2014, led the Seminoles offensively, and FSU was an outstanding defensive team, holding most of its opponents below sixty points per game.

Each team was thinking of that 2015 game, where Cuevas-Moore came off the bench to rally the Gamecocks early and Tiffany "Superwoman" Mitchell scored the biggest bucket of the season. But FSU was facing a much different USC team.

"They have tremendous players, and two of them have played in the ACC, with Kaela Davis and Allisha Gray. We have seen them for a number of years, and they are tremendous players," coach Sue Semrau said. "We recruited Tyasha Harris, a tremendous guard. I think you just go down the line, and they have a tremendous lineup. It's interesting that they are having to play a little bit differently now without Alaina Coates, but they are doing a great job with that. If you look at their postseason numbers, they are doing some great things."

But could they do it again? USC had only been in this position once and had advanced to the Final Four, but that was in basically a home game. Now this was as neutral a site as neutral could get. (Staley's complaints about being sent so far resonated. The game would have just 3,134 fans in attendance, and overall, the four NCAA regional sites' attendance figures were down 27 percent from 2016.)

Staley didn't ride her herd roughly. They were as relaxed as if the game was some meaningless exhibition. "I mean, you don't want them uptight. You know, they are kids. I want them to enjoy the moment," Staley said. "There is a time and a place for it all, and I want them to be comfortable. I want them to be loose. Because the team that gets to play at its normal composure is the team that is going to probably win the basketball game; that's closest to what they have played like all season long."

"This matchup, to me, it's going to help us redeem ourselves, like this is what I've personally been looking forward to for the longest, so I'm excited," Thomas said.

THE GAMECOCKS NEVER TRAILED, despite Wilson being in foul trouble and sitting for most of the two middle periods. Davis put the final stamp on a regional MVP performance with twenty-three points. USC again couldn't rebound, letting FSU grab an unsightly eighteen offensive boards. They coughed up the ball eighteen times, but they also shot nearly 58 percent with their biggest gun out of the game.

"We didn't want to take quick shots, so it almost played into our hands, minus the turnovers," Staley said. "So we ran the clock a little bit, and if that game is maybe five minutes longer, we could have a different result."

The one that was was plenty good enough. Gamecocks 71, Seminoles 64. USC was back in the Final Four.

"I came here to be in these games, to be in this situation," Davis said. "You know, I wouldn't want to be on another team and, you know, trying to get to the Final Four with another group of girls."

Thomas, also limited with foul trouble, scored eight points. The Gamecocks, like they seemingly always did, had trouble finishing the game, but the sixteen-point lead they built with 5:37 to go in the third held up.

Wilson scored four straight points after a turnover in the fourth quarter, but FSU kept coming, making it 65–62 after Brittany Brown stole a ball from Harris and laid it in. She redeemed herself by rebounding Gray's missed three-pointer and feeding Davis for a layup, and the Gamecocks again turned to Wilson.

The six-foot, five-inch All-American blocked two shots in the final twenty-six seconds, as FSU never got closer than four points. Forced to foul to extend the game, the Seminoles picked on Harris, who had missed those two crucial free throws late against Arizona State.

This time, the rookie swished both her attempts, and the Gamecocks were heading to Dallas.

Staley was in the Final Four for a fifth time. Waiting were Stanford, who the Gamecocks would play in the first semifinal, UConn (of course) and Mississippi State.

Would she finally win that elusive final game?

"That's why I left Temple to come to South Carolina to coach in the SEC with what I think is some of the greatest coaches in the game," she said. "And then you get to this stage at the Final Four, and then it's another tier of coaches who have won national championships, have won gold medals, have won a thousand games.

"I think I'm going to be amongst greatness and hopefully with that, you know, it will be a great experience with South Carolina."

OF COURSE IT WOULD be against someone she knew. Staley had been around far too long not to know the giants of women's college basketball.

Tara VanDerveer was not just a colleague.

"I feel like from my experiences with her, she taught me how to approach the game, how to approach pressure situations, and how to execute while being under that amount of pressure," Staley said. "[1996], that entire year, just opened my eyes to seeing basketball coached and played at a different level. The amount of pressure that was on our team, on Tara, she made us feel all of the pressure that was on her. She didn't want the team to fail."

Staley (along with USC assistant Nikki McCray-Penson and former USC assistant Carla McGhee) was on VanDerveer's Olympic squad that year, the latest to carry the banner for a team that had a strict motto: gold medal or you failed. VanDerveer led the team to another gold in its home country and continued to lead one of the most traditionally terrific teams in the country.

She won her 1,000th career game in 2016–17 and was hoping to win that elusive third national championship. Stanford had reached the Final Four seven times since winning it in 1992, which completed a run of two titles in three years, but had been blanked every time.

Then there was Staley, who had gone to three Final Fours as a player and lost and one as a coach and lost. The Gamecocks had also been eliminated in their first Sweet 16 by Stanford and in their second by North Carolina on Stanford's home floor. Something had to give.

"You know, the emotions, as I reflect on participating in the Final Fours, not being able to win a national championship is the thing that fuels me as a coach, to check that box off," Staley said. "Fortunately I've been around some great players to get us back at this point to compete for a national championship. Hopefully our day has come."

The Gamecocks were looking good and feeling confident. Despite not having Coates, the offense had really come around and covered the loss of rebounding and paint presence. Davis had found her shooting stroke and was carrying it into Dallas, and Wilson was the best player in the country, no matter what the votes for national player of the year said. (Washington's Kelsey Plum, who finished her career as the NCAA's all-time scoring leader, swept the national awards. Not discounting her accomplishments, but much of the voting was collected before the tournament began.)

"Once A'ja Wilson went down for a two-game period, we went to a smaller lineup, which helped us. When Coates went down, we just adjusted," Staley said. "We perfected the offense that worked for us. You're seeing us spread the floor a little bit, utilizing the talent that we have."

USC and Stanford tipped off, and the Gamecocks had twenty points at halftime. They scored six in the entire second quarter.

Where was this offense?

"Our energy was down, we just needed to play to our tempo, start pushing tempo," Gray said. "Once we got that, we got on our run."

A Harris steal midway through the third turned into a foul on Davis, sending her to the line for two free throws. She made both to cut Stanford's lead to five.

From there, it wasn't the prettiest basketball, as each team was socking the other with everything it had. Physicality and sparse points ruled, but the Gamecocks were starting to find a rhythm.

A defensive rebound and a layup from Gray pulled USC within one, and then Cuevas-Moore, as usual, shouldered the team in a postseason game. Her three-pointer splashed for a two-point Gamecock lead, and a jumper later pushed the lead to six.

USC stretched the lead to eight points with four minutes to play but hit the standard lull. Wilson and Davis each stole a ball only to turn it right back over, and when Alanna Smith canned a jumper, the lead was down to six. Smith nailed a three-pointer on the next possession, and it was once again gut-check time.

The Gamecocks had been here two years before and let it slip away. That team had Wilson but was led by Aleighsa Welch, Mitchell and other upperclassmen.

This time, it was Wilson's team. Like she had throughout the tournament, she took over. Her rebound of a Gray miss resulted in a foul and one made free throw. That was enough to turn it over to the guards. Harris and Cuevas-Moore took it home, 62–53.

The Gamecocks were in the national championship game.

"First of all, I just want to say to God be the glory that we're in this position, to play for a national championship. Something that is so very hard to do," Staley said. "Our team has an incredible focus on the end result. The stuff in between, it's going to happen. Runs are going to happen. Bad shots are going to happen. Turnovers are going to happen. But we hang our hats on being able to control some of the tempo that happens out there."

The Gamecocks and Cardinal played the early game. UConn and Mississippi State had the nightcap. USC would get a slight bit of advance prep, but big deal. The Gamecocks were going to play UConn.

The Huskies had won 111 straight games and the last four national championships. MSU had had a fine season but was encroaching on UConn's hallowed turf. The Gamecocks were already thinking of the past three years, where they'd been in games against UConn but lost all three. They'd never played them in the postseason but would get that chance in two days, for the only prize missing from Staley's trophy case.

It's not that USC didn't think it could beat UConn. Of course it did, of course it could. But it wasn't just playing the Huskies' collection of All-Americans, it was playing that mystique. UConn doesn't lose. Like, ever.

They'd never say it, but everybody in that locker room was pulling for Mississippi State to spring the upset. The Gamecocks weren't discounting the Bulldogs if they somehow pulled it off, because it would obviously mean a great team advanced to the national final over an impossible-to-beat opponent. Yet they were familiar with the Bulldogs, having beaten them twice that season and handling them every time during MSU's rise from good to strong to elite, and wouldn't their chances of winning the title be increased against a team they already knew?

Fat chance of that happening. It's UConn. But there was still hope.

All they needed was one itty-bitty miracle.

13

MEANT TO BE

K aela Davis was relieved South Carolina figured out a way to beat Stanford and advance to the national championship game but was apprehensive about that national championship game. Frankly, the Gamecocks hadn't been sharp against the Cardinal, and if they were going to complete their journey, to take this thing back home with them, they couldn't afford another bad night.

"We came out flat and didn't play a good game. I think that spoke to how good of a team we were and how well we knew each other that we were able to pull that game out," Davis said. "For us, we were just like, 'It doesn't matter who we play, we want to get back on this floor and play better.' You want to play UConn and get that rematch, but we just wanted to get back on the floor more than playing a specific opponent."

The coaches stayed for the entire next game—Mississippi State versus Connecticut—but the players watched the first half in the arena and left. They went back to the hotel to rest, eat and get ready for their final practice, and then final game, of the season.

The Gamecocks weren't pulling for one team over the other, although most would assume they'd naturally want Mississippi State to win. USC felt it could beat anybody, but playing the Big Blue, going for its fifth straight national title? Man, would that be a high hurdle to clear.

So they relaxed and watched a great game unfold and didn't pull for one over the other. Really, they didn't.

"It honestly didn't matter who we played," Allisha Gray said. "We were just focused on going out there and preparing for the game."

Brad Muller had packed up his gear and was about to take his family to get a bite to eat. He saw the first quarter courtside and watched the rest from the restaurant.

Like most, he applauded the Bulldogs for their start. But it surely wouldn't last.

"Part of me was waiting for UConn to make its run that it had always made over the last four years. Having seen them play a lot of very good teams, including South Carolina, there were plenty of teams that could play with Connecticut for four quarters, but Connecticut would always go on a run," Muller said. "You always had to wonder, 'Who was going to counter?'"

Mississippi State was playing the game of its life. The crowd at Dallas's American Airlines Center was agog over the battle, for while the Bulldogs were an excellent team, the opponent was UConn. UConn had won the last four national championships, among its eleven total, by far the most in women's basketball and tying UCLA in the men's game. UConn had gone an incredible 111 straight games without a loss dating to a 2014 defeat at Stanford—which pushed South Carolina to its first No. 1 national ranking—and included three wins over the Gamecocks and a sixty-point cutting of Mississippi State in the 2016 Sweet 16.

The Huskies seemed tired and unprepared for what the Bulldogs would throw at them, which was defense first, second, third and fourth. They couldn't get their normal fluid offense to work as MSU built a nine-point lead at the end of the first quarter and swelled it to sixteen early in the second.

Yet everybody knew what was going to happen, because it's UConn. They'd figure out whatever was wrong, reel off one of those patented UConn runs and dance into yet another national championship game.

Sure enough, they did—mostly. After taking that sixteen-point lead, MSU missed five shots and twice turned the ball over in less than four minutes. The lead was sliced to four points. Thanks for a great quarter-and-a-half, ladies.

But MSU responded, repairing its offense and defense in the *thwip* of the nylon basket. Victoria Vivians swished a jumper to stop the bleeding, and MSU extended the lead to eight points by halftime, refusing to give up and accept what most—OK, what everyone—saw as inevitable.

"You see, you have to be careful when you start talking about people that you really don't know about. If all you're doing is evaluating what you see on TV, and you don't really know what's inside somebody's breastplate, you better be careful about evaluating them," MSU coach Vic Schaefer said. "That's what these kids have. They have tremendous heart. They also have a little pride. We had our pride stepped on last year by another great team, just like that one today."

It had been a stirring half, but nobody was thinking upset. Twenty minutes could feel like an hour against UConn's galaxy of stars. When Napheesa Collier drained a shot for the Huskies' first lead at 6:14 of the third, the MSU fans who traveled to Dallas, a crowd that also included Dallas Cowboys quarterback and MSU alum Dak Prescott, sighed. It had been one hell of a season, but the Bulldogs were going to again fall just short of a championship. It happened in the SEC regular season; it happened in the SEC tournament.

"As the game went into the second half, MSU was hanging around, that's when I felt they had a chance. I knew they were very good, but when UConn didn't pull away, I felt something might be up," Muller said. "I said to a few people before, 'Morgan William is one of my favorite players to watch when she's not playing us.' Had to love somebody who could play like she can. As it got to the fourth, I thought, 'UConn doesn't have a lot of these games.' And then I thought that MSU had talked all year about wanting to get UConn again and prove it was much, much better than that sixty-point whipping they had last year."

MSU refused to play its scripted part. The Bulldogs stayed patient in their sets, never feeling the pressure to immediately try to equal a UConn bucket. The offensive lulls that hampered them all season were left in the past.

The lead went back and forth, neither team able to take a two-possession lead until Vivians scored in the paint to make it 56–52 Dogs, 3:57 to play. Of course UConn's Katie Lou Samuelson nailed a three-pointer right after, but now the crowd and the announcers were starting to think it, even if they didn't necessarily believe it. Could this actually happen?

UConn was putting it away as Gabby Williams finished in the lane for a three-point lead, but Vivians immediately took it back with a free throw and a three-pointer. Ahead one point with seventy-four seconds to play, MSU just needed a stop, a shot, some kind of break to pull off one of the greatest table-turners in NCAA history.

They got it from an unlikely place. Morgan "Itty Bitty" William, the diminutive guard who spurred Mississippi State with massive performances throughout the tournament, stole the ball with less than a minute to go. Dribbling time, she threw up the game-winner with twenty-seven seconds showing—but missed, Collier hauling in the rebound while MSU's Breanna Richardson fouled her.

That was it. Collier had two shots and MSU was going to lose. UConn players never, ever folded in these kind of situations; rumor had it coach Geno Auriemma spent entire practices on "clutch" situations since his players had regular basketball down pat.

Collier missed the first free throw. The arena was shocked. She made her second to tie the game at sixty, but MSU was going to have a chance to win this thing on the last shot.

William's last effort was blocked and rebounded by Gabby Williams as the horn blew. Free basketball.

Who wants it more? Who believes more?

No one scored for nearly the first ninety seconds of overtime. Richardson aced two free throws for the lead, UConn tied it. Teaira McCowan finished a layup for the lead, 1:12 to play, then had a ball come right to her after Williams fumbled it away.

Hoping for the coffin nail, Blair Schaefer launched a three-pointer with thirty-one seconds to go, but it missed, Samuelson gobbling the board and calling timeout. The Huskies, with their own past greats in the stands (Breanna Stewart, Maya Moore and Sue Bird), needed two to tie, three to win. MSU didn't have a great idea of who the ball was going to—there were simply too many options—so Vic Schaefer made it simple: play defense the way we know how.

Dominique Dillingham followed Samuelson into the lane as she was looking to finish a high pass with a tying layup. Never taking her eyes off the ball, the five-foot, nine-inch Dillingham reached up to snare the ball, her elbow colliding with the six-foot, three-inch Samuelson's chin. It was not intentional at all. It was a basketball play.

The officials whistled Dillingham for a flagrant foul.

Schaefer went ballistic, as did most of the country. UConn might very well win anyway, but here was the game being handed to them.

"There was a collision underneath the basket. Lou went flying out-of-bounds. They looked at the monitor, and they said she got hit with an elbow or a forearm in the face or something," Auriemma said. "By rules, they have to call that. I don't know why they didn't call it when it happened. They were standing right there."

The lateness of the call and review made it worse. There was no way that was intentional, but contact had been made. Samuelson was given two free throws, and of course she made them to tie the game, twenty-six seconds to play.

Schaefer had to be walked back to his sideline by his assistants. Considering the horrendous call that just cost his team the lead, he's lucky the refs didn't tag him for a technical foul as well.

But livid as he was, he managed to relax.

"Once the coach kind of calmed down a little bit, we got 'em back together," Schaefer joked. "I said, 'Hey, fine. This is right up our alley, ending the game on a defensive stop. Let's go make a stop.'"

MSU believed and then saw it nearly end one more time. Dillingham turned the ball over, and now UConn would have the last shot.

But Saniya Chong didn't wait for the last second. She ran from the right wing, William picking her up as she penetrated the lane. William set up to take a charge, took the bump, went down and saw Chong's shot fly untouched out of bounds.

Foul? There was contact there. The way this was going, of course William would be called for the foul and Chong would have two shots.

But it didn't happen. Nor did Chong get called for a charge. It was a UConn turnover, MSU ball, twelve seconds to go.

Dillingham dribbled up top as time went down, hoping for a last shot or easy pass to Vivians or McCowan. William came to her, taking the handoff, saw the clock hit four seconds and ran.

She flashed to the right wing as Williams came to her. William planted, lifted, shot the ball toward the rim, trying to aim it as well as she could from the brief glimpse she received before Williams stretched out her arm trying to block it.

The buzzer sounded. The glass turned red.

William's shot, one that was heard around the country but especially in Storrs, Connecticut, fell perfectly into the basket.

Itty Bitty turned, eyes closed and mouth screaming, her fists on her waist. She was swallowed by her jubilant teammates as Auriemma could only smile. "When it went in, it was almost like, 'Of course. Of course, it's going to go in,'" he said.

The streak was over. UConn was slain. It would be an all-SEC national championship game, Mississippi State and South Carolina meeting for the third time of the season.

"I had no doubt Morgan was going to take the last shot. When it left her hands, I knew it was going in," Muller said. "I remember thinking two things: 'Wow, that was a piece of history!' because everybody will always remember who broke UConn's streak. Then I thought, 'Dang, we gotta play these guys again?' We already had two knockdown drag-outs with this team, because I'm sure our team probably thought, 'We're gonna get UConn again.'"

"It was crazy, absolutely crazy when she hit that shot," Davis said. "I remember I called it, I remember I said, 'That's good.' In my mind, I wasn't even thinking yet, 'OK, we play Mississippi State.'"

Schaefer picked up William in a bear hug and cradled her like a newborn, still disbelieving the shot had gone. Starkville, Mississippi, rejoiced as its never-say-die band of warriors just pulled off an upset for the ages.

Columbia, South Carolina, channeled the thoughts of many.

"We just won the national championship."

THE GAMECOCKS THEMSELVES DIDN'T think that. They couldn't afford to think that. Let the others say what they want, but Mississippi State was coming off the biggest win in its history and the biggest win in women's college basketball in years. The Bulldogs had momentum and would have an awful lot of people pulling for them to finish the run with a national championship.

USC knew how tough MSU was. The Gamecocks had played them twice already. They won each, the last time without Alaina Coates just like they'd have to this time, but they weren't going to accept any conversations about relaxing just because they wouldn't have to play UConn.

Yet the unspoken vibe was present—"This is the best chance we're ever going to have."

"It does make it easier [that we've played them before], but you can't—for what Mississippi State has done over the past five games, you know, they're much different than they were that game in which we played them in the SEC tournament championship," Dawn Staley said. "They're playing at an all-time high."

Yet there was some thought, maybe just a word or two in passing conversation. At practice the day before the game, Muller was a little worried that Mississippi State was on such a clear emotional high. That changed when he overheard a few tidbits.

"[USC] felt good about it. No disrespect to Mississippi State, but I think they felt they were going to beat whomever they played. It was that kind of confidence. A staffer said, 'We got better players and we're gonna win.' I believed them."

"We broke down a lot of film, what made us successful and not so successful, what things we could differently," Davis said. "At the end of the day, we knew what we had to do and a lot of it was the same things. That's what's so hard about playing a team for the third time in a season is you have to do those same things to be successful. Can you do it?"

"You're confident in your team no matter what. National championship game?" Gray said. "You're going to be confident that your team will win regardless of who you play."

Muller's nervousness began to ebb the more he thought about it. While never one to say, "Oh yeah, it's in the bag. No question," he had been around this team since Staley arrived.

The Gamecocks had more talented teams, more talented players. But this team had that bond that it wasn't going to be defeated, especially now that it was so close. Others could say not playing UConn was a once-in-a-lifetime break, but Muller thought the Gamecocks, even though they lost to UConn in February, would find a way to win even if they had played the Huskies.

"I think South Carolina was so motivated that even though they'd been good for a few years by then, they still played that underdog role. They had played well for a period up in Storrs, but this team in particular wasn't intimidated by the thought of playing UConn, even for a national championship," Muller said. "This team thought it was their time. They had been playing so well, and without Alaina Coates, that they felt they could handle anything. They had me convinced going into the Final Four that they were going to beat UConn."

The pregame routine didn't change a dribble. USC held shootaround, a meal, a departure time from the hotel as steady as it had been throughout the tournament. As the Gamecocks came through the lobby, of course their fans were waiting in a two-column line to high-five and wish their heroes luck, but USC was as stony as the monuments on Easter Island.

Staley wasn't going to say anything to upset her team's mentality, and if she was thinking of her own championship failures, she didn't show it. She simply spoke about doing what got them here, of playing South Carolina basketball, as she gathered her team together.

"She was calm. For her first championship game appearance, she handled it well," Davis said. "I know everybody on the inside was probably screaming, but she played it cool. Our thing was, 'Let's go have a parade.' Everybody kind of stuck that in the back of their head."

Muller was waiting for his standard pregame interview, recorded an hour before tipoff and played on the air about fifteen minutes before. As poker-faced as Staley could be before a game, she had a tell. Muller knew how good she felt about the possibility of winning by her reaction to the interview.

"I'm going to ask four questions. If she's feeling really good, the answer's going to be more than three minutes. If she's feeling pretty good, it's going to be three minutes. If she's a little concerned, it's going to be 2:30, 2:45. If it's less than 2:30, we're in trouble," Muller said. "But her pregame interview that day went pretty well. I looked at the timer walking back to my seat and said, 'We're going to be OK.' Because if Dawn feels good about it, barring something unforeseen like two girls rolling their ankles in the first quarter, we got it."

THE GAMECOCKS AGAIN STARTED slow, and Mississippi State again started fast. The Bulldogs led 7–1 before USC worked out the jitters and took an 18–14 lead at the end of the first. Davis missed her first two shots, but Gray was two for four for six points, while A'ja Wilson had four points on two shots and already had two steals.

The Gamecocks padded their lead as the Bulldogs again went through an offensive lull, unable to match USC bucket for bucket and often ceding three scores to their one. At halftime, USC led by ten, and the parade was being planned.

Something didn't feel right on Mississippi State's bench. While the Bulldogs had their issues with gaps in scoring all year, they felt they could handle USC this time. The problem was USC had posted a lengthy winning streak over the Bulldogs by doing exactly what it was doing in this game.

The Gamecocks always contained MSU's stars. They could handle Vivians and William and affect the six-foot, seven-inch McCowan like not many opponents could. They never found an answer for Dillingham, but Dillingham wasn't the kind of player who could win the game by herself. She'd score five to fifteen points and that'd be it.

But MSU had come too far to go away this quietly. The lead swelled to fourteen before the Bulldogs came back. They scored nine straight to make it 45–40 with 3:39 to go in the third, and when Davis missed another jumper but it became a flurry of missed MSU shots, the Gamecocks returned to what they had been all year.

Gray picked off a pass and scored on a layup. The period ended with back-to-back Wilson and Davis buckets, and USC led 52–44.

Ten minutes. Ten minutes for everything the Gamecocks had fought for. Ten minutes to finally end Staley's quarter-century quest for a championship.

There was simply no way Wilson would let her coach and team down. The woman who put MSU away in the SEC tournament, saying afterward that in a championship scenario, the player who wants it the most wins, won one more time.

The junior scored eight points with three rebounds and two blocks in the final ten minutes, taking over the game after MSU again cut the deficit to six points. The rest of the Gamecocks picked up their pace as Schaefer did the unthinkable.

William, the hero of the tournament, didn't play in the fourth quarter. She didn't have a great game—two for six for eight points and four assists—but after being the Bulldogs' spine for five games, she wasn't playing the most crucial part of the sixth. Her replacement, Jazzmun Holmes, played and played well, but she wasn't William.

"Jazz was playing good today," Schaefer said. "Morgan, she had some struggles early. I thought we had a couple kids today that just didn't quite have the energy level that we needed. Plus, when you got somebody maybe that seems like they're a little tired, you're trying to give 'em a blow. Next thing you know, the person you're putting in is playing pretty good. Maybe you don't want to take 'em out."

Vivians scored twelve points but was four of sixteen from the floor. The Bulldogs fought but couldn't overcome Gray (eighteen points), Davis (ten) and Wilson (the MVP).

The clock hit 3:10.

Muller doesn't script his calls. Not many announcers do, preferring the emotion to be off the cuff. Plus, what happens if you have this great call planned and then somebody hits a circus shot and you have to talk about that instead of the words you labored over? Might as well not make the effort.

As the clock wound down, Muller thought about what he'd say.

"Every year, Dawn did something greater, something better. To me, that was the natural conclusion," he said. "The year before, we had run the table in the SEC, so you couldn't do better than that. But we had a bad finish in the NCAA tournament, so this year, I thought we'd do better. The game starts, and State went on a couple of runs, but we always countered. At that point, I thought, 'Our players aren't going to let us lose.' Mississippi State was darn good, but we were really good."

TIFFANY MITCHELL WAS FRANTICALLY trying to get her phone to pick up Russian Wi-Fi while standing in the freezing weather outside the airport, waiting for her luggage. Playing overseas is a thrilling adventure, but the logistics sometimes…

She finally got a signal and saw USC ahead by ten, and there was not much time for an MSU comeback. The player, the "Superwoman" who saved so many games for USC, knew it was about to happen.

"I felt like we had championship teams at least two of the four years I was there. We lost by a point in one Final Four—it still hurts me to talk about it," she said. "I feel like that was our chance, that opportunity and it got away from us. It's hard to live that twice. I'm glad they didn't have to do that."

IN HER NATIVE TRENTON, La'Keisha Sutton thought of all the times she wouldn't let her coaches and teammates see her cry. She had to be tougher, be the leader, be the one who wouldn't accept defeat, but it was often difficult to keep that inside.

As the Gamecocks closed in on the title, she couldn't stop it.

"I was crying my freaking eyes out. I was literally crying, and the whole family was cheering, high-fiving, they looked at me, 'Keisha, are you crying?' I was literally at a loss for words."

All of the heartbreak, the desperation to win, the decision to come back after wanting so badly to succeed and the one beautiful season at the end returned at that moment. This was why she came back. This was what she started.

"I'm happy for the girls and Dawn, and sad personally," she said. "I always felt like we could compete and win championships. It was just hard when I was there."

ALEIGHSA WELCH WAS PLAYING professionally in Portugal and hoping she could pick up the TV feed when it came time. Leading up to it, she felt a little regret on two parts. One, like Mitchell, she was that close to a championship in 2015 and felt Notre Dame was the one that got away.

Two, she wanted UConn.

"I felt like everything fell into place the way it should have. Would I have loved to see them beat UConn? Of course! You want to avenge those losses," Welch said. "But give MSU credit, we played them twice and they're tough."

Welch was in her room, watching on the computer, but when the fourth quarter began, she asked her teammates if she could plug it into the TV in the den. They said sure and then saw their roomie explode.

"I was crazy. Jumping up and down, screaming, I don't think they've ever seen more pure joy than when that buzzer went off," Welch said. "I didn't cry. I had to put my big-girl pants on there. But I texted everybody that night."

MULLER THOUGHT OF STALEY'S acceptance speech to the Naismith Memorial Basketball Hall of Fame as he kept calling the action while thinking what he'd say in the final thirty seconds. "It was about what Dawn had built and the first thing I thought of was, barring a last-second shot to where you have to talk about that, was her hall of fame induction speech. And how she said something to the effect of, 'Follow me as we win a national championship at South Carolina,'" Muller said. "At the time, we were happy to be in the Sweet 16. I didn't doubt her, but that just seemed far off. She got kids that were talented and believed in her, and she did it. I wanted to work it in during the fourth quarter."

1:35: "Dawn Staley, when she was enshrined in the Naismith Basketball Hall of Fame back in 2013, talked about winning a national championship here at South Carolina, and she has never backed away from that. Gamecock fans have embraced it. And now the Gamecock players—the student-athletes—are trying to deliver just that."

0:10: "Fly your garnet and black, Gamecock Nation. This is *your* time! The South Carolina Gamecocks are on top of the basketball world! They will cut down the nets and bring them back to South Carolina as the 2017 national champions! There's the horn! The Gamecocks rush the floor. When Dawn Staley was enshrined in the Naismith Basketball Hall of Fame in 2013, she talked about winning a national championship at South Carolina. She promised. Gamecock Nation believed. And today, the Gamecocks have delivered. What a ride! The Gamecocks are national champions! They defeat Mississippi State 67–55 as the confetti falls here in Dallas!"

Dawn Staley was—at last—a national champion.

14

FORWARD MARCH

She clutched the trophy she had waited so long to hold, the freshly snipped net around her neck. Neither would leave her sight much longer than a night for the next two months.

"It means that I can check off one of the things that has been a void in my career. It's one of two opportunities that I saw women play for when I was younger—national championship games and Olympics," Dawn Staley said. "Those were the things that I held dear and near to me when I was growing up, because those are the things that I wanted. That's what I saw. That's what I was shooting for."

She finally had it. After so many close finishes as a player, after so many days at Temple where she constructed a tournament team but couldn't get further than just making the tournament, after so many bad early days at South Carolina to bad days ending great years at South Carolina.

Again, she never saw herself coaching. Now that she'd been in it seventeen years and had the only bauble she had never obtained, she could never leave.

"I really can't see myself doing anything other than what I'm doing, impacting the lives of young people, and also being able to check this box off in my career," she said. "I'm really grateful and thankful that [Dave O'Brien] made this possible."

Nobody ever questioned her greatness as a coach, but the championship put her into exalted territory. As an athlete, Staley knew full well the blessing and the curse of winning "a ring." Marginal players who sat at the end of the bench sometimes got one, while some of the game's greatest somehow didn't.

Like Jim Boeheim and Gary Williams said when they won theirs, Staley didn't necessarily think she was a better coach than she was before the championship game. But she knew she'd entered that privileged status, that behind-the-velvet-rope club of the Ring.

There was no "but" beside the name anymore. The girl from Philly who was raised on a basketball court now owned the courts of the nation. Coming to a program lost, in need of something, anything to have hope of just a winning season someday, Staley transformed a hardscrabble bunch of believers into a talent-dripping squad that was now the best team in America.

"I mean, I'm going to enjoy it. It's something that I've been coaching for seventeen years now. I played college basketball, what, twenty-five to twenty-eight years ago? It took that long," Staley said. "But I also want people to know that just because something takes a long time, you have to have patience, you have to persevere, stay with it. If something is a goal of yours to accomplish, you don't give up on it.

"I never gave up on winning a national championship, no matter how hard it was, no matter what it looked like. I'm just so happy that I get a chance to share it with so many different people in my coaching, basketball family tree. Coaches, former players, mentors, everybody."

THEY LINED THE SIDEWALKS of Columbia's Main Street, wearing their garnet and black and holding pennants, hand-made signs or distributed posters. All said the same—"National champs!"—or a variance of it.

National championships haven't happened very often at South Carolina, but when they have, they normally get a parade down Main Street toward the statehouse, where they're greeted by the ancient dome flying three flags: American, South Carolina and the USC flag reserved for special occasions.

There was nothing more special than Staley's team bringing home the title. The fans who accumulated the best attendance totals in the country over the past three years would in no way be denied showing up one more time.

"I don't think there are words to really describe that moment," said Kaela Davis, who transferred from Georgia Tech strictly because she wanted to win a national championship. "But that was our thing, we wanted to do it for all those fans that had been there for us in highs and lows and in-betweens. It was really cool for us to see all those people representing for us at that moment."

Alaina Coates was able to climb aboard a float for the parade, despite her foot cocooned in a cast. The rest of the newly crowned champions, with trophy and nets, were on top of a bus as it slowly motored down Columbia's tree-lined drag.

From far away, the ones who helped start this run beamed.

"I'm honored, I'm grateful because they didn't have to offer me a scholarship, let alone keep me. They could have stacked more and more McDonald's All-Americans better than me. Since I left, people ask me, 'Where you from?,'" said La'Keisha Sutton. "I'll say Trenton, but it makes me proud that I also say, 'South Carolina.' I'm proud of what we did. We did win a championship. I'm honored to be able to say I played for the University of South Carolina under Dawn Staley."

"To be the last standing is something that we've all tried very hard to accomplish. It just so happened to happen at a place that really appreciates our sport, really supports our sport like no other, and it couldn't happen to a better fan base than ours. We've had many things happen to our program that people may have looked at as a loss. What happened to our program throughout the years really set us up to win a national championship this past season," Aleighsa Welch said. "What a national championship team looks like, sounds like, feels like…it didn't at first feel that way with this team for one reason or another, but they made it what they wanted it to be."

Staley would have a section of street near Colonial Life Arena christened in her honor, where her name joined Frank McGuire's as fabled USC basketball coaches. She would wear the net from the game, calling it her "net-lace" to rival A'ja Wilson's constant string of pearls, for most of the next thirty days.

She thanked the fans who lined the streets, filled the courtyard and swarmed the statehouse steps. It was an absolute joy to reward them with what they first thought possible, then saw as realistic and ultimately knew they would no doubt one day win it.

Their hopes mimicked her journey. It certainly wasn't easy, but she had done it. At South Carolina, of all places, she had done it.

"I'm on the float, my wife and son are with me, I'm seeing thousands of people I don't know, but there are some I do know, and I remember when I walked to the podium and seeing that sea of garnet and black. I thought, 'Holy cow. Nobody does this!'" play-by-play man Brad Muller said. "The UConns and Tennessees and Baylors and Texas A&Ms, whoever won championships might have had celebrations, but nothing like that. It was just joy. It didn't matter what you thought about Democrats or Republicans or any of that, for that day, everybody was on the same team, and it was awesome."

"That was the most fun I've had in Columbia, to see the fans that have been supporting us all year and to be able to bring a national championship to them," said Allisha Gray, who left one national championship program in the hope she could win one at a place that never had. "They do so much for us and helped us win several games in the Colonial, so it was just great to be able to celebrate with them."

Staley said it right then—she was so, so glad to have that title, but she didn't want to rest on it. It was time to win more, to be greedy. Why couldn't South Carolina be the next Connecticut, to win so many championships people are stunned when they don't win it?

"Obviously if you start winning, and they start believing in your program, they're going to come. That's what took place. I'd like to think, you know, we got an incredible marketing department, and we do, but you can market women's basketball all you want, all you want. If people don't believe in the product that's on the floor, they're not going to come.

"I just think our fans believe in the product. We make them feel a part of our program. We talk to them. We invite them to our offices. We put on events just for them. In return, you know, they become No. 1 in attendance for the past three years, which is unheard of in South Carolina, what people think of as a football town."

COATES WAS A SENIOR and was drafted second overall by the Chicago Sky. Tiffany "Slim" Davis also graduated. Davis and Gray, eligible and coming off their greatest accomplishment as college players, decided to bypass their final years of eligibility and head to the WNBA. Gray was picked fourth by Dallas, Davis tenth, also by Dallas.

USC lost a lot of firepower but stood to return Wilson, two-time SEC Player of the Year, first-team All-American and a sure bet for 2018 National Player of the Year. Bianca Cuevas-Moore and Tyasha Harris would return at point guard, Alexis Jennings would be free after sitting out her transfer year and Doniyah Cliney would be back to help lead a suddenly young team.

The three now-sophomores, including Harris, could welcome a class of newbies, another highly ranked group of recruits that included three freshmen and two transfers. They would take a summer trip to scrimmage the Japan women's national team, getting a crash course in Staley's new systems and how they would attack and revamp following a national championship season.

The trophy Staley desired sat on the desk of the women's basketball offices in Columbia, a few feet from the giant crystal basketball enshrined in its own case in the lobby, just down the walkway from another overflowing trophy case. Staley's accomplishments speak for themselves, but if anyone needed a reminder, well, just look.

It would definitely be a different team in 2017–18.

But the Gamecocks had dealt with player losses and player additions before while they constructed a national champion.

It's why Staley was following the same script she always had when given ten days of practice before leaving for Japan. Rookies and veterans gathered around as she calmly explained what she wanted out of a particular drill. All nodded as Staley broke the huddle.

Here we go.

ACKNOWLEDGEMENTS

I was in Phoenix watching South Carolina come back to beat Stanford and advance to its first national championship game and never felt more guilty.

In a perfect storm of events, the Gamecocks' men's team shocked the planet by advancing to its first Final Four, and I was with them every step of the way. I had been there for all of Dawn Staley's postseason trips, even writing on a men's coaching search during the women's first postseason in West Lafayette, Indiana, but I was missing this one.

You spend as much time as I have around a team or coach and you want them to do well. I was pleased to see the Gamecocks keep winning but felt bad about not being there.

Yet Staley understood, with a hearty greeting on the floor in Dallas while we both brushed confetti out of our hair. I was able to get out of Phoenix that morning and get to Texas for tipoff, walking in the arena with my laptop bag over one shoulder and duffel in hand. I'm extremely glad I was able to see her finally get her national championship.

My deepest thanks to Staley, her players and staff over the past nine years, for answering my questions and being accessible. Without them, this book would clearly have been impossible.

I also wish to thank:

- Rick Millians, Mark Lett and the staff at *The State* for aiding me in this venture. Josh Kendall, Ben Breiner and Matt Connolly filled in for me during postseason games, while Tracy Glantz, as always, stored the moments with her camera.

- USC women's basketball sports information director Diana Koval, for her assistance in media relations through the past nine years.
- Brian Shoemaker of GamecockCentral.com, who allowed me to write about women's basketball when not many readers or fans were interested.
- The fans, who have never been shy about reaching out and saying hello, and have made Colonial Life Arena the best women's atmosphere in the country.
- Kevin, who encouraged me to be a full-time sportswriter. The long hours and unpredictability can be hard to deal with, but I know now, as he knew then, that I could never be happy doing anything else.
- Rick, my sounding board for all things Gamecock—and all other things.
- My mother and father, for always being there.
- Marjorie. Nothing I do matters without you.

INDEX

ABOUT THE AUTHOR

David Cloninger has covered South Carolina athletics off and on since 1996. He has covered Gamecock basketball and Dawn Staley's teams full-time for the past nine years for three media outlets. Cloninger lives in Columbia.